THE STRANGER

THE GREENHAVEN PRESS
Literary Companion
TO WORLD LITERATURE

READINGS ON

THE STRANGER

Derek C. Maus, *Book Editor*

David L. Bender, *Publisher*
Bruno Leone, *Executive Editor*
Bonnie Szumski, *Series Editor*

Greenhaven Press, Inc., San Diego, CA

Library of Congress Cataloging-in-Publication Data

Readings on The stranger /Derek C. Maus, book editor.
        p. cm. — (The Greenhaven Press literary
companion to world literature)
    Includes bibliographical references and index.
    ISBN 0-7377-0565-5 (pbk. : alk. paper) —
ISBN 0-7377-0566-3 (lib. bdg. : alk. paper)
    1. Camus, Albert, 1913–1960. Etranger. I. Maus,
Derek C. II. Series.

PQ2605.A3734 E8645 2001
843'.914—dc21

                                        00-061730

Copyright © 2001 by Greenhaven Press, Inc.
PO Box 289009
San Diego, CA 92198-9009
Printed in the U.S.A.

My work will count as many forms as it has stages on the way to an unrewarded perfection. The Stranger *is the zero point. . . . The last point will be the saint, but he will have his arithmetical value, measurable like man.*

—Camus, from a 1942 notebook entry

CONTENTS

FOREWORD

"'Tis the good reader that
makes the good book."

Ralph Waldo Emerson

The story's bare facts are simple: The captain, an old and scarred seafarer, walks with a peg leg made of whale ivory. He relentlessly drives his crew to hunt the world's oceans for the great white whale that crippled him. After a long search, the ship encounters the whale and a fierce battle ensues. Finally the captain drives his harpoon into the whale, but the harpoon line catches the captain about the neck and drags him to his death.

A simple story, a straightforward plot—yet, since the 1851 publication of Herman Melville's *Moby-Dick*, readers and critics have found many meanings in the struggle between Captain Ahab and the whale. To some, the novel is a cautionary tale that depicts how Ahab's obsession with revenge leads to his insanity and death. Others believe that the whale represents the unknowable secrets of the universe and that Ahab is a tragic hero who dares to challenge fate by attempting to discover this knowledge. Perhaps Melville intended Ahab as a criticism of Americans' tendency to become involved in well-intentioned but irrational causes. Or did Melville model Ahab after himself, letting his fictional character express his anger at what he perceived as a cruel and distant god?

Although literary critics disagree over the meaning of *Moby-Dick*, readers do not need to choose one particular interpretation in order to gain an understanding of Melville's novel. Instead, by examining various analyses, they can gain numerous insights into the issues that lie under the surface of the basic plot. Studying the writings of literary critics can also aid readers in making their own assessments of *Moby-Dick* and other literary works and in developing analytical thinking skills.

The Greenhaven Literary Companion Series was created with these goals in mind. Designed for young adults, this unique anthology series provides an engaging and comprehensive introduction to literary analysis and criticism. The essays included in the Literary Companion Series are chosen for their accessibility to a young adult audience and are expertly edited in consideration of both the reading and comprehension levels of this audience. In addition, each essay is introduced by a concise summation that presents the contributing writer's main themes and insights. Every anthology in the Literary Companion Series contains a varied selection of critical essays that cover a wide time span and express diverse views. Wherever possible, primary sources are represented through excerpts from authors' notebooks, letters, and journals and through contemporary criticism.

Each title in the Literary Companion Series pays careful consideration to the historical context of the particular author or literary work. In-depth biographies and detailed chronologies reveal important aspects of authors' lives and emphasize the historical events and social milieu that influenced their writings. To facilitate further research, every anthology includes primary and secondary source bibliographies of articles and/or books selected for their suitability for young adults. These engaging features make the Greenhaven Literary Companion series ideal for introducing students to literary analysis in the classroom or as a library resource for young adults researching the world's great authors and literature.

Exceptional in its focus on young adults, the Greenhaven Literary Companion Series strives to present literary criticism in a compelling and accessible format. Every title in the series is intended to spark readers' interest in leading American and world authors, to help them broaden their understanding of literature, and to encourage them to formulate their own analyses of the literary works that they read. It is the editors' hope that young adult readers will find these anthologies to be true companions in their study of literature.

INTRODUCTION

The Stranger is not a book that strikes readers with an overwhelming initial impression. This slim volume, narrated in a simple and straightforward style, does not attempt to draw its readers in with verbal pyrotechnics, structural complexity, or lyrical power. The story meanders along, a particularly unusual pace given the shortness of the book. A large number of readers have no doubt drawn near the halfway point of the book and wondered if Meursault was ever going to *do* anything. To further confound those expecting a conventional novel, the climax of the action occurs near the middle of the book and in the space of less than three pages, passing by so rapidly that it is possible to overlook it.

Why then is it that readers around the world have made (and continue to make) *The Stranger* one of the most widely read pieces of literature of the twentieth century? Published in 1942, *The Stranger* on one level provides insight into the psychology of a specific time and place, namely Algeria prior to World War II. However, the novel also deals with a question that has recurred universally in literature dating back to ancient times: "What, if anything, does my existence mean?" Like most writers who preceded him, Camus does not answer this question. Nevertheless, the process of asking the question and sorting out the ramifications of the potential answers provides him with the building blocks to create a work of art whose power seems undiminished more than a half-century after its initial appearance.

Critical responses to *The Stranger* are plentiful and interpretations of the novel's meaning are wide-ranging. The selections included in this book represent only a few of the angles from which Camus's readers have attempted to penetrate a novel that remains as enigmatic as its narrator. From those who read *The Stranger* as a work of cultural history to those who see it as one of the cornerstones of modern existentialist philosophy, the story of the stoic Meursault has generated a wealth of opinion about the meaning of a book that repeatedly denies the validity of making meaning out of the world. Far from being an irreconcilable paradox, this characteristic is what makes the novel a masterful work of art.

Although Camus certainly intended the reader to feel some sympathy for Meursault—he repeatedly explained and defended his protagonist in the years after the book was published—it is also important to remember that Meursault was not created as an infallible character. Though he is sacrificed by his creator to make a point about the absurdity of the society in which he was placed, Meursault is not a martyr. Camus himself wrote of Meursault in the introduction to a later printing of *The Stranger:*

> One would therefore not be much mistaken to read *The Stranger* as the story of a man who, without any heroics, agrees to die for the truth. I also happen to say . . . that I had tried to draw in my character the only Christ we deserve.

The creation of such an unheroic and fully human Christ-figure underscores Camus's belief that truth is a matter of introspective reflection (such as Meursault undergoes while awaiting execution) rather than social, religious, or legal decree.

Ultimately, the beauty of *The Stranger* is its ability to spur this sort of self-examination in its readers. The viewpoints in this book generally represent the individual truths that their authors have arrived at after contemplating the novel. Thus, one should not be surprised if they do not always agree. The views presented here are more a chorus of voices than a monotone. They all suggest possible ways in which one can interpret *The Stranger*, just as Meursault's contemplation in the prison cell gives him the opportunity to examine the various potential truths before him.

A Biography of Albert Camus

On November 7, 1913, less than a year before the outbreak of World War I, a French-Algerian vineyard worker named Lucien Camus and his wife, Catherine, celebrated the birth of their second son. They named the boy Albert, since the first son (born three years earlier) had already been named Lucien after his father. The family lived in Mondovi, a small village in the Algerian interior where the elder Lucien found ample, if not particularly profitable, work. Albert's mother was of Spanish descent, having been born Catherine Sintès (a surname that will recur in *The Stranger*). She had been hearing- and speech-impaired since early childhood as a result of an untreated illness and worked as a cleaning woman at the time of Albert's birth.

The infant Albert was born into a tumultuous country within an increasingly tumultuous world. Algeria had been a French colony since its conquest in 1830 and the population was a mixture of Arabs, Berbers (the indigenous North African population), French, Spanish, Greeks, Italians, Maltese, and Jews. Albert's own ethnic background—half-French, half-Spanish, born in Algeria—placed him in the category of the *pied-noir*, a French term literally meaning "black foot" but used to describe individuals of European, especially French, descent born in Algeria. These various components of Algerian society existed in a state of uneasy truce at the time of Albert's birth, but the difficulties arising from the French colonial policy toward the Arab and Berber population of Algeria would quickly become (and remain) an important issue for Albert.

War and violence on an even larger scale would profoundly affect Albert's life before he was even conscious of it. His father succumbed to serious wounds suffered during the first Battle of the Marne in northern France in October 1914. Albert never knew his father and learned only a few passing details about him from his mother over the course of his later life. Nevertheless, the loss of his father at a very early age helped steer Camus toward a personal philosophy that abhorred war and violence in general. Unfortunately for him, the massive upheavals in both his native Algeria and in Europe during the course of his lifetime frequently put him in positions where violence seemed almost unavoidable, forcing him to abandon his essentially pacifist principles. Camus's life and writings are dominated by themes that spring from both his sensitivity toward ethnicity and his fervent dislike of violence and death.

CHILDHOOD AND ADOLESCENCE

After Lucien Camus was called to military service in July 1914, his wife was faced with the daunting prospect of trying to survive in Mondovi without her husband's income. Deciding that this was not feasible, she and her two young sons moved in with her mother, Maria Sintès. Madame Sintès lived in a four-room apartment above a wine shop in the working-class Belcourt neighborhood of Algiers with her two sons Joseph and Etienne. The six of them lived together in extremely cramped and impoverished conditions. Camus's mother worked long hours as a charwoman to provide for the family while Madame Sintès saw to the upbringing of her grandsons in her particularly stern and occasionally cruel manner.

Camus himself had some fond memories of his time in Belcourt despite the privations brought on by the war and by his family's poverty. He perceived his Belcourt roots as a badge of genuine working-class origins as well as a place in which he got firsthand experience of Arab and Berber life. The neighborhood contained a thorough mixture of ethnicities, although the French were the dominant group (unsurprisingly, since Algeria was technically a part of France at the time). Despite conflicts among these groups that flared up occasionally, Belcourt proved to be a home in which the young Camus found some measure of happiness. Patrick McCarthy, one of Camus's many biographers, writes:

> Belcourt influenced Camus in two ways. Living on the streets, he had to fend for himself. He enjoyed the company of other boys but he also knew how to fight them off. He acquired that mental boxer's stance which his friends would notice; he learned to be wary and to counterpunch. He also acquired a sense of community. There was a warmth about Belcourt which went beyond the taunts which the French and Spanish hurled at each other....

The curious Camus considered Belcourt his territory and he explored it. As a young boy he knew all the café-owners and the shopkeepers. Long after he left Belcourt he would seek out the working-class neighbourhoods in the cities he visited. He loathed New York, but enjoyed Chinatown in lower Manhattan because he rediscovered there the "teeming street life" which he had known in his childhood.[1]

Whatever benefits there may have been in Belcourt for Camus's later development as a thinker and an artist, life in his grandmother's apartment was harsh. His mother was often thoroughly exhausted when she returned from work in the evening and could not provide the attention that her fatherless sons naturally sought from her. His uncle Etienne was a hard worker who helped support the family, but he too was deaf and occasionally prone to abusive behavior, especially toward Camus's mother. Madame Sintès was a severe disciplinarian who berated Camus's mother for having married a man who died and left her alone to raise two children. She was largely uninterested in the intellectual development of either Lucien or Albert, preferring to prepare them in her own way for a life of hard work and self-discipline. While Camus loved his family, he was very different from them—largely because of his literacy—and found relief only through his schooling.

He started school in 1918 and within a few years his industrious nature had gained the attention of a dedicated teacher named Louis Germain. Germain saw great potential in his young pupil and encouraged him greatly in his studies. In the spring of 1924, when the time came for Camus to take the entrance exam for high school, Germain personally attended to his preparations. Camus's mother approached Germain before the exams and told him that she could not afford to pay for her son's education beyond elementary school. Her older son Lucien had already taken a job after an undistinguished elementary school career and Madame Sintès insisted strongly that Albert go to work as well. Much of the expense of his elementary schooling had been paid for by a stipend given to him as the son of a war casualty, but this money did not apply to high school. When Germain assured Camus's mother that Albert would win a scholarship that would provide for books and meals (the schooling itself was free), she somewhat cautiously agreed to allow him to take the test. He passed it with distinction and bore out Germain's prediction, winning a scholarship to attend the high school in the nearby district of Bab-el-Oued.

He started school there in October 1924, taking classes including Latin and French, which was considered the usual preparation for a schoolteacher. He made a number of friends at school who would remain important figures in his life and was by all accounts an outgoing pupil who was intellectually and physically active. He read voraciously, especially from books provided to him by his uncle Gustave Acault (the husband of his mother's sister Antoinette), with whom he began to associate regularly as he advanced in school. Acault was a butcher by profession, but indulged his intellectual interests on the side. He provided young Albert with books by such authors as Fyodor Dostoyevsky, Anatole France, and, most importantly, the French socialist writer André Gide. Gide would later become Camus's friend and colleague, but it was Acault who introduced his nephew to Gide's writing in 1929.

Camus was an athlete of significant renown during his time in school at Bab-el-Oued, swimming regularly at the many beaches Algiers had to offer and starring as the goalkeeper for the junior squad of the Racing Universitaire Algérois (RUA) soccer team. His circle of friends included not only a number of up-and-coming writers and artists but also a great number of people he knew from the soccer fields. Camus wrote many years later about the positive influence of soccer on his development: "After many years during which I saw many things, what I know most surely about morality and the duty of man I owe to sport, and learned it in the RUA."[2]

Camus was forced to give up athletics when he first fell ill with tuberculosis, a disease that would stay with him for the remainder of his life. He was diagnosed with the disease in his right lung late in 1930 or early in 1931 (the exact date is unclear, as is the case with many of the details of Camus's early life) and spent several months recuperating, both in the hospital and in the Acaults' home, to which he had moved. The family agreed that the comparatively wealthy Acaults could better provide for the convalescent Camus's needs. Gustave Acault readily agreed to take his nephew in.

Beginning in fall 1930, Camus had begun taking philosophy classes from Jean Grenier, a recent French émigré to Algeria who rapidly became the next important academic influence in Camus's life. Grenier had achieved moderate success as a writer of philosophical sketches in France before moving to Algeria, but it was his mentoring of Camus during and after the period of his first bout with tuberculosis that shaped Camus's development as a thinker and as an artist.

Camus was forced to repeat his final year of high school to make up the time he had missed due to his illness, but this also meant that he had another year to soak up the contemporary French literary and sociopolitical writing that filled Grenier's bookshelves, especially that which appeared in the important left-wing journal *Nouvelle Revue Française* (*New French Review*). His grandmother died during this year, an event that considerably lessened the pressure on him to take up a "practical" profession at the conclusion of his school years. He passed the *baccalauréat* (the final examination required for admittance to higher education in the French system) in June 1932 and sought admission to the University of Algiers at Grenier's urging.

COLLEGE, COMMUNISM, AND SIMONE

Even before he started classes at the university, Camus had begun publishing articles in a local publication called *Sud* (*South*). These early pieces demonstrate a keen mind and Camus began to think of himself as a professional writer. He produced three articles on a broad range of topics including poetry, philosophy, and musicology, areas in which Grenier's instruction had been influential. He continued to write a number of short pieces for various journals throughout the remainder of his college days, a practice that prepared him for his later, more substantial journalistic work.

Camus spent the 1932–33 school year in a program of study known as *hypokhâgne* (neither the word nor the concept has an easy English equivalent). This year was generally intended to be spent taking courses specifically in preparation for university-level work. In addition to his normal course of study, he sat in on courses at the university and engaged in private intellectual debates with Grenier and with his friends Max-Pol Fouchet, Claude de Fréminville, André Belamich, and others. He also became romantically involved with Simone Hié, a young woman who associated with a number of his fellow students.

Simone was the daughter of a well-to-do Algerian family. She had been addicted to morphine since the age of fourteen (she was sixteen when Camus met her). She was Fouchet's girlfriend when Camus first made her acquaintance in 1930—notably, at a celebration of the centennial of France's conquest of Algeria—but he would gradually fall in love with her over the course of the next four years before marrying her on June 16, 1934. Simone's somewhat wild lifestyle was in sharp contrast to the generally reserved Algerian manner, especially that of most of Camus's peers, so she seemed exotic and adult to Camus despite the fact that he was slightly older than she was. He also believed he was capable of rescuing her from her serious drug problems, a stance that few of his friends and none of his relatives (especially Gustave Acault) shared. Furthermore, Simone's abandonment of Fouchet for Camus drove that previously close pair of friends apart irreparably. At the time of their wedding, though, Camus felt that this marriage was right for him.

By the time of their marriage, Camus had matriculated at the University of Algiers and was active in a number of groups on campus that opposed both the rising Fascist movement in Europe (Hitler and Mussolini had solidified their respective holds on power in Germany and Italy and the Spanish Civil War was not far off) and the general mistreatment of workers and the poor in Algeria by the ruling classes. Although he would not officially join the Algerian Communist Party until 1935, he worked extensively for a number of causes supported by the more radical left wing. He was joined in these activities by a great number of his friends, almost all of whom were politically active as well, since this had become a standard by which Camus measured his acquaintances.

Even as he continued his successful studies at the university, he spent greater and greater amounts of time organizing groups of students in activities designed to work against the injustices he perceived in the world. He suffered a relapse of tuberculosis in late 1934. While this allowed Camus to avoid the compulsory military service for which he was due, it also drastically limited his ability to work and provide for himself and his new wife. The financial support the young couple had received from both her parents and the Acaults quickly evaporated—in large part due to Simone's continuing morphine consumption—and the marriage quickly turned sour.

Simone was rumored to be sleeping with unscrupulous young doctors in exchange for morphine prescriptions, which so upset Camus that they decided together that she should go away to the Balearic Islands of Spain to escape the lures of Algeria. Camus joined her several months later and they returned to Algiers with renewed hope of patching up their marriage. Simone quickly relapsed into her old habits, though. She entered a drug treatment clinic in Algiers briefly but was unsuccessful in ridding herself of her addiction.

In large part to distract himself from the problems with his marriage, Camus threw himself wholeheartedly into his schoolwork and his political endeavors. He finished his coursework in 1935 and spent the next year writing a lengthy thesis under the guidance of Grenier (who was teaching at the university by this time) and another professor, René Poirier. In his thesis, Camus compared the ideas of the pre-Christian Greek philosopher Plotinus with those of the early Christian scholar Augustine of Hippo (St. Augustine). He received his diploma in late May 1936 after defending his thesis cum laude. The normal course of action for him would have been to go on to teach, but Camus's bad health prevented him from qualifying for the necessary certification. This eventuality freed him for what he had come to see as his true vocation anyway, namely writing.

Soon after joining the Communist Party in fall 1935, he was named secretary-general of the newly formed Maison de Culture (House of Culture), an organization intended to bring intellectual and political education to the working classes through the arts. In this capacity, he helped found the Théâtre du Travail (Theater of Work) and became deeply involved with this company as an actor, director, writer, and producer. He decided that theater was the best means for him to spread his political beliefs and found a group of collaborators in the Théâtre du Travail with whom he could satisfy this desire.

His marriage to Simone disintegrated in summer 1936 after a disastrous trip to Austria, Germany, and Czechoslovakia. Camus, Simone, and a mutual friend, Yves Bourgeois, had set out on a trip through Europe after the completion of Camus's thesis. The trip was marked by Camus's apparent discovery of a letter to Simone from a doctor in Algiers that intimated a drugs-for-sex relationship between them. Camus traveled separately from Bourgeois and Simone for more than a week afterward and the relationship between Camus and Simone was icy during the remaining month of the trip. His notebooks do not provide much insight into his feelings, but the following entry from late July is telling for its sense of his disillusionment: "Married couples: the man tries to shine before a third person. Immediately, his wife says: 'But you're just the same . . .' and tries to bring him down, to make him share her mediocrity."[3]

When they returned to Algiers in September, Camus moved in with his brother and Simone went to live with her mother. They would not divorce for four more years, but the marriage had, for all intents and purposes, ended.

SUCCESS, DISILLUSIONMENT, AND SUCCESS AGAIN

The more Camus's personal life faltered, the more he threw himself into his work with the Théâtre du Travail. The group's first production, an adaptation of André Malraux's short novel *Days of Wrath*, had been a rousing success among the lower classes of Algiers in January 1936. Camus had been in charge of the production and was invigorated by the positive reaction to the innovative way in which the play had been staged. The sets had been highly stylized and sparse (in part due to the lack of funding that plagued the group) and the audience had literally been made a part of the performance. The second production was supposed to have been a play written collectively by the group (although subsequent readers claim to have discerned the overwhelming influence of Camus on the text) based on a workers' uprising in Oviedo, Spain, in 1934. The play was banned before it was performed, however, by the mayor of Algiers, presumably because of its radical subject matter. Portions of the play were performed under a different title and the script was published in May 1936 by a sympathetic young publisher, Edmond Charlot.

When Camus returned from the ill-fated trip to Europe, the group began rehearsing an adaptation of *The Lower Depths* by the Russian playwright Maxim Gorky. Camus simultaneously worked in a number of menial jobs to support himself at this time and had moved in with a number of his fellow actors and artists in a large, dilapidated villa overlooking the ocean called the Maison Fichu, but nicknamed the House Above the World by its inhabitants. *The Lower Depths* opened in November 1936 and was followed by productions of *Epicene* by Ben Jonson, *Prometheus Bound* by Aeschylus, *Article 330* by Georges Courteline, and *Don Juan* by Aleksandr Pushkin. Camus himself played the lead role in the last of these, a somewhat fitting casting given Camus's wide-ranging appetite for female companionship in the years following the demise of his marriage.

Early in 1937, Camus found work acting with Radio-Algiers. He toured with the network's acting group and traveled to small towns throughout Algeria with the troupe, putting on plays by renowned eighteenth-century French playwrights such as Molière and Beaumarchais. He also tutored students privately and found small jobs to make money, all of which exhausted him and caused a relapse of his tuberculosis late in the spring.

Despite bad health and numerous distractions, Camus managed to organize and revise a number of his political and philosophical essays into a collection published by his friend Charlot in May 1937. Although published in an edition of only 350 copies, *The Wrong Side and the Right Side* marked Camus's first large-scale publication and helped reinforce his belief that he could and should be a writer professionally. It took two years for the copies to sell out and it did not meet with a sizable critical reception, but Camus was proud of his work and determined to write more.

After his illness returned, he traveled for a month and a half during the summer of 1937 to France and Italy with his close friend Claude de Fréminville. They visited the Provence region of France and then moved on to Paris, which Camus had always thought of visiting but had yet to see. After this, Camus moved on to Florence, which he immediately and deeply loved. During the week he spent there, he toured the monastery in the hilltop town of Fiesole and recorded his thoughts in the notebook that he had begun keeping two years earlier. Camus returned to Algeria in mid-September and began working on the draft of a novel called *A Happy Death.*

He thought briefly about taking a job as a teacher in Sidi bel-Abbés, a small town in the Algerian countryside, and actually went to work there for a day before deciding to return to Algiers. Almost immediately on his return to Algiers, he became embroiled in a dispute within the Communist Party concerning the role of the Muslim Arab population. The leadership of the party wanted to distance themselves from Arab issues, preferring to focus on the economic concerns of those of European origins in the working class. This position was contrary to Camus's notion of what communism should achieve, but he found it difficult to convince a large enough portion of the leadership that the abandonment of the Arabs was disgraceful. He left the party in November 1937, taking a number of his colleagues with him and essentially dooming the House of Culture and Théâtre du Travail.

He wasted no time after his break with the Communists, though. He almost immediately founded the Théâtre de L'Equipe, an acting troupe consisting of a large portion of the Théâtre du Travail group. He also found a job through a friend working as a meteorology observer. This job provided him with a steady enough income to devote time to both his new theater and to his writing. During the course of 1938, he began working on manuscripts that eventually became *The Stranger, The Myth of Sisyphus,* and the play *Caligula.* In addition to working on the production of several other plays, Camus acted the part of Ivan Karamazov in the Théâtre de L'Equipe's adaptation of Dostoyevsky's *Brothers Karamazov.*

CAMUS AS JOURNALIST

In late 1938 he left his job at the meteorology office and began working for *Alger-Républicain,* a new left-wing paper under the editorship of Pascal Pia. Pia was an unorthodox but politically committed journalist who moved from France to take over this new publication. His friends included writers like Malraux and Gide, both of whom Camus respected greatly, so Camus looked forward intensely to meeting and working with Pia. The two would become very close friends within months of making each other's acquaintance and would work together on journalistic projects for almost a decade before a falling out in the late 1940s.

When *Alger-Républicain* began publishing in October 1938, Camus quickly became intricately involved in the writing and production of the daily newspaper, the only one in Algiers that represented a leftist viewpoint. Camus wrote a regular literary criticism column; one of the new works he reviewed was *Nausea* by Jean-Paul Sartre, who would later become Camus's friend and intellectual rival. Additionally, he reported—in a highly critical voice—on a number of important trials around Algeria and wrote a series of investigative reports on the administration of the Kabylia region, where a serious famine was in progress in the summer of 1939. He worked long days, usually together with Pia, laying out the pages and reading page proofs in the small office that housed the newspaper.

Even as he was quickly acclimating to the job of journalist, he was working on his fictional and philosophical writings. In May 1939, Charlot published *Nuptials*, a collection of four lyrical prose pieces, including Camus's recollections of Florence. He also continued to work on two novels, a play, and a philosophical treatise.

In addition to his growing artistic and literary standing, Camus had also rightly acquired a reputation as a seducer by this time. He had begun a relationship with Francine Faure, a student of mathematics at the University of Algiers, but he also spent a considerable amount of his scant free time in the cafés of Algiers admiring and occasionally pursuing women. His relationship with Francine was marked from the beginning by alternations between Camus's natural sense of romance and a growing distrust of love stemming from his bad experiences with Simone.

Pia and Camus quickly made *Alger-Républicain* into an important voice of dissent, but their task was made more difficult by the outbreak of World War II in September 1939. Camus was strongly opposed to war at the time, vehemently denying the necessity of fighting, even in the face of aggressive fascism. He attempted to enlist in the military, apparently out of a desire to persuade other soldiers to refuse to fight. He was rejected on the grounds of his health and used his position on the editorial board of *Alger-Républicain* to publish articles and editorials critical of the growing military sentiment. Camus wrote the following in his notebook on September 7, 1939:

> It is always useless to cut oneself off, even from other people's cruelty and stupidity. You can't say: "I don't know about it." There is nothing less excusable than war, and the appeal to national hatreds. But once war has come, it is both cowardly and useless to try to stand on one side under the pretext that one is not responsible. Ivory towers are down. Indulgence is forbidden—for oneself as well as other people.
>
> It is both impossible and immoral to judge an event from outside. One keeps the right to hold this absurd misfortune in contempt only by remaining inside it.[4]

His contempt for the war changed only after France was overrun by Germany the following summer.

The imminent onset of war had caused *Alger-Républicain* to come under military censorship in July 1939, a situation that led to its eventual banning by the government in January 1940. Although Pia and Camus actively resisted the limitations on what they could print, they courted their own disaster by printing, among other things, a number of pieces that were severely critical of French colonial policy in North Africa. The fact that these were printed during a time in which the stresses of war made any local conflict a potential powderkeg led the government to close down the newspaper, leaving Pia and Camus out of work. Pia immediately returned to France and got a job with an evening newspaper in Paris called *Paris-Soir*. Pia sent word to Camus that a job for him might open up at *Paris-Soir* soon, and Camus began making plans to move north.

He moved to Paris in March 1940, taking on the job of editorial secretary with the newspaper and living in a small apartment in the historically bohemian Montmartre district. He quickly became alienated in Paris, unhappy to be separated from the Algerian climate to which he had become accustomed and feeling trapped in a dirty and inhuman city. He wrote in his notebook:

> What is hateful in Paris: tenderness, feelings, a hideous sentimentality that sees everything beautiful as pretty and everything pretty as beautiful. The tenderness and despair accompany the murky skies, the shining roofs and endless rain.[5]

By June, he escaped the gloom of Paris, but not by choice. The Germans were threatening to overrun the city as the staff of the newspaper fled to unoccupied regions of the country, stopping first in Clermont-Ferrand (roughly 150 miles to the south) and then moving on to Lyon in September.

His divorce from Simone had been finalized earlier in the year and he and Francine decided to marry late in 1940. She joined him in Lyon and they were married December 3 in a simple civil ceremony. Within a month of their marriage, though, Camus lost his job, as *Paris-Soir* cut its staff to reduce expenses. Since he had only been there a short time, he was not retained. With no reason to remain in France, Camus and his new wife returned to Algeria early in January 1941, moving into Francine's family apartment in Oran, 250 miles from Algiers.

Altogether, they spent eighteen months in Oran, although Camus traveled regularly to Algiers on business or to visit his old circle of friends (and, occasionally, girlfriends). He did some work as a reader for his former publisher Charlot, but this did not provide much income. He worked as much as he could on his three unfinished manuscripts. He eventually found steady employment as a private teacher for Jewish students who had been expelled from the school system under the so-called Vichy (named after its capital) government of defeated France. Camus detested this regime for its collaboration with the Nazis and found that educating the direct victims of its policies was a means of fighting it. He disliked Oran, finding it provincial and intolerably hot. The fact that his in-laws, especially Francine's mother, viewed him with distrust and occasional dislike further fueled his desire to leave. Finally, a serious relapse of his tuberculosis (this time affecting his left lung as well as his right) forced him to depart for the Faure family's vacation retreat in France at Le Panelier, a small town in the Massif Central mountain range southeast of Lyon. Little did he know that he would never call Algeria home again.

CAMUS AND THE RESISTANCE

Less than a month before he left Algeria, Camus's career as a writer took a dramatic turn for the better when the Parisian publisher Éditions Gallimard released *The Stranger* on July 11, 1942. Despite the difficult conditions of the occupation, a combination of clever deception and occasional unpleasant cooperation with the Germans allowed the Gallimard family to keep their publishing house operational throughout the war years. They had been influential in the production of the innovative literary journal *Nouvelle Revue Française*, which Camus had eagerly read since first meeting Grenier more than a decade earlier, and published books by many of the rising talents in French literature. Bolstered in part by a positive review by Jean-Paul Sartre (who had himself not yet achieved the cultural stature that he soon would win) the book quickly became a minor sensation. It suffered from small printings due to chronic wartime paper shortages, but Camus's name was well recognized not long after he settled in Le Panelier.

In October 1942 Francine returned to Algeria intending to find work for herself and her husband. Strengthened by the hearty food and clean air of the mountains, Camus intended to join her by the end of November but wanted to stay at Le Panelier as long as possible. His delay proved to be too long, as a surprise Allied invasion of North Africa (code-named Operation Torch) began on November 7 and was followed by a German invasion of southern France that placed Camus and Francine on opposite sides of impassable battle lines.

With no job and no connection to his family in Algeria, Camus was faced with a difficult situation. Although his philosophical treatise *The Myth of Sisyphus* had been published by Gallimard in mid-October 1942, the money he had received as an advance for it and *The Stranger* was long gone. He managed to piece various small writing jobs together to make money. He lived in Le Panelier until November 1943, making regular trips to Lyon and Paris to meet with his growing circle of literary friends. On one trip to Paris in January, he met Spanish actress Maria Casarès, with whom he would soon begin an affair that lingered on-and-off for the rest of his life.

Although his life was far from comfortable, Camus was able to sustain himself during this year and worked on finishing *Caligula* as well as starting work on another play, *The Misunderstanding*, and a novel that would later become *The Plague*. He also began contributing a number of pieces to publications affiliated with the French Resistance, although many of them were uncredited for reasons of personal safety. He was not officially affiliated with the Resistance until late 1943 or early 1944 (because of the lack of documentation the exact date is hard to determine), by which time he had moved to Paris and was on collegial terms with important intellectual figures such as Sartre and his lover Simone de Beauvoir, Malraux, Jean Paulhan, and others.

With Pia's assistance, Camus got a job as an editorial reader for Gallimard, a position he would hold for the remainder of his life (although it was at times little more than a title), and moved to Paris in November 1943. Also through Pia's influence, Camus started writing for the underground newspaper *Combat*, which was produced by an influential group of French loyalists led by Claude Bourdet. Camus's biographer Herbert Lottman describes *Combat* as follows:

> At best the newspaper was a drop in the bucket. Produced in danger, with the risk of arrest, torture, and imprisonment or execution, it could only serve to lift morale a mite; it could not change the course of the war. Could it change the postwar world? For active resistance workers, such as those of the Combat movement, were laboring not only to rid their country of enemy troops and of a collaborationist government; if they were making sacrifices to free France, it was because they also hoped to make a better France after the liberation.[6]

This high-minded goal corresponded closely with Camus's ideas about the social and political responsibility of writers. Although he now accepted the need for violence to defeat the threat of fascism, Camus wanted this effort not simply to restore the prewar status quo, but to effect a positive cultural change instead. He saw *Combat* as a golden opportunity to do just that, in addition to placing him in contact with similarly minded individuals.

During the first half of 1944, Camus became a committed member of the Resistance, not only writing articles for *Combat* but also taking part in clandestine activities like hiding dissidents and smuggling information out of Paris. His affair with Maria Casarès intensified as the year went on and Camus fell deeply in love with her during the production of his play *The Misunderstanding*, in which she played the lead role. The play opened in June 1944, three weeks after D-day and less than two months before the Germans would be forced to retreat from the city in the wake of the Allied military advance. Although the reviews were mixed, the play bolstered Camus's reputation, in part because of the euphoria surrounding liberation.

After Allied troops marched into Paris on August 25, 1944, *Combat* quickly became an openly published newspaper and maintained a very high profile for the next several years. Camus, Pia, Sartre, Gide, Malraux, and others worked for the paper during this period and their contributions helped make *Combat* the prime leftist voice after liberation. Gallimard also published the scripts of *The Misunderstanding* and *Caligula*, which Camus had finally revised to his satisfaction.

Once Paris was freed from occupation, Francine was free to rejoin her husband and arrived in the city in mid-October. Camus and Maria continued seeing each other for a few months, but she eventually rejected his offer to continue the affair. When Francine announced that she was pregnant early in 1945, Maria and Camus broke off their relationship, intending the break to be permanent.

This separation was hard for Camus, who had become dependent on Maria for both artistic and romantic companionship. Maria was the exiled daughter of a former prime minister of Spain and her familial connection to a prominent anti-Fascist made her all the more attractive to Camus. Although Camus was by most accounts devoted to his wife, he continued to have a number of extramarital affairs until his death. In September 1944 he wrote in his journal:

> Those who love all women are those who are on their way to-ward abstraction. They go beyond this world, however it may seem. For they turn away from the particular, from the individual case. The man who would flee all thought, all abstraction, the truly desperate one, is the man of a single woman. Through persistence in that singular face which cannot satisfy everything.[7]

The birth of his twin children, Jean and Catherine, on September 5, 1945, temporarily renewed Camus's resolve to be a faithful husband to Francine, but he strayed again within a matter of months.

After the War

Camus kept himself busy with a number of projects during the two years following the end of World War II. In addition to writing and editing for *Combat,* he also continued work on the manuscript of the novel that eventually became *The Plague* and started writing his third play, *State of Siege.* His first play, *Caligula,* had finally been produced, opening in Paris on September 26, 1945, but it was not well received. Audiences and reviewers alike found Camus's drama, based on the life of the violent and possibly insane Roman emperor Caligula, overly grim and somewhat inaccessible. Camus considered his new set of works (*State of Siege, The Plague,* and the philosophical essay *The Rebel*) a response to and refinement of his initial threesome of works (*The Stranger, The Myth of Sisyphus,* and *Caligula*), which he nicknamed "the absurds."

His position at Gallimard had become more important as well. He was placed in charge of a new series of publications entitled *Espoir* (*Hope*) and used it to publish a number of works by writers whose views he shared, including several of his close friends from Algeria and the Resistance. Camus was an exceptionally loyal and committed editor, as Lottmann points out:

> At Gallimard the editor did not work as he might in some other French houses (and in all American publishing firms), following the book from the receipt of the manuscript to publication. . . . But Camus did interest himself in the editorial problems a manuscript might present. . . .
>
> Perhaps this wouldn't be considered as much editing in the publishing worlds of New York or of London, but for Paris of

the time, and for Gallimard, it represented more than usual dedication. Another young author discovered that Camus'[s] suggestions were directed to what the author could do best, not what Camus himself would have done.[8]

In March 1946, Camus was sent to the United States as an emissary of the French Ministry of Foreign Affairs on what was essentially a cultural public relations tour. Despite a brief dispute with immigration officials upon his entry—the result of Camus's refusal to answer questions about his political affiliation—his trip would be the catalyst for his transformation into a literary superstar. *The Stranger* was published in an English translation on April 11 and immediately became a success again. American newspapers were filled with accounts of the moody leftist French author with the uncanny resemblance to actor Humphrey Bogart. The press linked him frequently with Sartre, uniting the two under the banner of "existentialist" writing. Camus vehemently denied the connection, stating that, unlike Sartre, he did not claim to have the answers to everything. Camus spent two months living in New York and speaking at a number of college campuses, most notably Columbia University. Although he was largely unimpressed with what he saw in the United States, he did find a number of French émigré companions who made his stay tolerable.

He returned to France in June and settled in to finish writing *The Plague*. The idea for this work had come to him in Oran almost six years earlier, but his work had proceeded slowly in the meantime. He scaled back his work with *Combat* but socialized frequently in what were often lengthy drinking binges with Sartre, de Beauvoir, Gide, and Arthur Koestler, among others. Between his return from America and *The Plague*'s publication in June 1947, Camus suffered another major relapse of tuberculosis, left *Combat* after an increasing series of political disagreements with his old friend Pia, and argued more frequently and angrily with Sartre. All of these events began to isolate him—physically, philosophically, and emotionally—from a large portion of the group of people with whom he had been close for the better part of the last decade. Despite the immediate and enormous success of *The Plague*, which brought him financial stability and even wealth for the first time in his life, Camus suffered from depression and poor physical health for most of the next two years.

He spent 1948 traveling extensively, to Switzerland, Algeria, England, Scotland, and southern France. He worked on finishing *State of Siege,* as well as starting another play entitled *The Just Assassins* and continuing work on *The Rebel.* He also encountered Maria Casarès again by chance and their romance soon resumed, as did her participation in Camus's theater work. She was selected for a part in *State of Siege* and was part of the cast when that play opened a brief and wholly unsuccessful run on October 27, 1948. For the next eleven years, Maria and Camus intermittently carried on their affair, with Maria at least as important a female presence in Camus's life as Francine.

In June 1949, Camus was once again sent abroad by the Ministry of Foreign Affairs, this time to Latin America. Although he met with enthusiastic audiences wherever he went, he was exhausted by the grueling travel schedule. Additionally, he suffered from depression at his separation from both his family and from Maria. By the time he returned to France in August, he was primed for a relapse of tuberculosis and found himself bedridden for much of the fall and winter.

Late in 1949, his play about Russian revolutionaries in 1905, entitled *The Just Assassins,* opened in Paris, again with Maria Casarès in a leading role. The play fared somewhat better than *State of Siege* but still failed to engage audiences in the way that Camus's fiction and journalism had.

The openness of Camus's affair with Maria began taking its toll on his marriage, although Camus himself seems to have believed that continuing both was possible. In a notebook from late 1948 he remarked:

> People insist on confusing marriage and love on the one hand, happiness and love on the other. But there is nothing in common. This is why it happens, the lack of love being more frequent than love, that some marriages are happy.[9]

By 1950, it was apparent to most of Camus's acquaintances that he was in love with Maria and married to Francine. The stress of this situation eventually caused Francine to suffer from nervous illness for several years in the mid-1950s and many of Camus's biographers have criticized him at length for his unwillingness to change his ways to potentially relieve her distress.

TROUBLED TIMES BEFORE *THE FALL*

Although his reputation had suffered mildly from the mixed reception of his past two plays, Camus was still an important figure in French literature. He published a collection of his political writings, including many of the pieces he had written for *Combat*, as *Actuelles I*. He spent much of 1950 and early 1951 in southern France, working diligently on *The Rebel* and attempting to recover from his most recent tuberculosis relapse. His health kept him from maintaining the level of activity he was used to and he fell out of touch with a number of his former Parisian friends, especially Sartre.

The Rebel was published in October 1951 and Sartre wasted little time in publishing a scathing review of it in his magazine, *Les Temps Modernes* (*Modern Times*). Written by Sartre's protégé Francis Jeanson, this review accused Camus of having withdrawn from real revolutionary ideals by criticizing certain aspects of communism (such as Stalin's massive system of labor camps). Camus replied in a seventeen-page letter that was printed in the magazine that Jeanson (and, by extension, Sartre) had deliberately misrepresented his ideas because of Jeanson's own lack of tangible experience with class struggle. Finally, Sartre applied the coup de grâce to both his intellectual association and friendship with Camus by responding to his letter with an angry personal attack of more than twenty pages in the August 1952 issue. The two leading figures of French leftist thought had clearly parted ways—leading many who were friendly with both to choose between them in subsequent years—an event that made headlines throughout the world.

Although he produced no major new literary works during the next few years, Camus remained active. He devoted himself occasionally to political causes, especially the growing unrest in his native Algeria. He began translating and/or adapting for the stage a number of foreign novels (such as William Faulkner's *Requiem for a Nun* and Dostoyevsky's *The Possessed*), as well as traveling extensively in Algeria, Italy, and Greece. He had been planning a trip to Greece since before the outbreak of World War II and he was overjoyed to finally achieve this goal in April 1955. Despite the onset of Francine's mysterious illness in summer 1953 and its worsening throughout the following year, Camus spent long periods of time away from his family with Maria Casarès. He also worked on editing and revising his second collection of journalistic pieces (*Actuelles II*, published in late 1953) and his final book of lyrical reflections (*Summer*, published in spring 1954).

Late in 1954, tensions between the Arab Muslims and the *pied-noirs* in Algeria boiled over and Camus found himself caught in the middle. Although he had formerly supported the Arabs in their struggle for civil rights, he saw their leaders in 1954 as violent and power-hungry individuals who were using the ethnic and class unrest to their own advantage. However, the actions of the French-Algerians were often equally reprehensible to him and he found himself reduced to the ineffective role of mediator between two groups with no wish to mediate. As the conflict grew worse, Camus's sense of helplessness grew and he feared for the safety of his aging mother and of his remaining friends in Algeria.

Much of his next novel, *The Fall*, was based on his experiences in relation to the Algerian uprising. It takes the form of a five-day conversation between the narrator and a Parisian lawyer named Clamence in which the latter tells a philosophical version of his life story. Many of the details that Clamence relates over the course of the five days parallel events in Camus's own life, leading most critics to interpret the book as at least semiautobiographical. Camus had initially conceived of it as a short story to be included in the collection *Exile and the Kingdom*, on which he had been working sporadically since 1952. It grew quickly into a more lengthy work that was published in May 1956.

Camus's notoriety at that time had been based more on his participation in the Algerian unrest than on his literary output, and he had angered French intellectuals on both the political right and left with his apparent unwillingness to support either side. *The Fall* reestablished his place in French literature, both in terms of its popular success and because it refocused the attention of his readers on his artistic skill. Critical praise was equally forthcoming and most likely led to his receipt of the Nobel Prize the following year.

Not long after the publication of *The Fall*, Camus moved out of the house he shared with Francine and their two adolescent children. Although they did not legally separate, this action clearly marked the dominance of Camus's more public life over his private life as a father and husband. Lottmann describes some of the difficulties in this arrangement:

> Camus managed to spend a month each year (at least a month), during school holidays with his children. He was conscious of his role as a father, and of his twins' need of a father. . . .

Camus and his wife took pains to minimize the celebrity of Albert Camus the writer, but their father's fame gradually filtered through. Once, when Camus was angry at his son over a domestic incident and ordered him from the dinner table and to bed, Jean walked off mumbling: "Good night, minor writer of no importance."[10]

THE NOBEL PRIZE AND CAMUS'S FINAL YEARS

Nineteen-fifty-seven proved to be a busy year for Camus. His direction of the production of his adaptation of *Requiem for a Nun* was an unqualified success. It played to full houses almost nightly from its opening in September 1956 through its close in January 1958. He published *Exile and the Kingdom,* his collection of short stories on the theme of exile, in spring 1957. He also contributed an essay entitled "Reflections on the Guillotine" to a work produced in collaboration with Arthur Koestler that called for an end to capital punishment. In addition, he worked on the draft of another novel entitled *The First Man* and continued his adaptation of *The Possessed.* Although he had once again suffered a relapse of tuberculosis late in 1956, it was not as severe as previous attacks had been and he worked ceaselessly for most of the year.

In October 1957, he was informed that he had won the Nobel Prize in literature, an announcement that he greeted by stating that Malraux should have won instead. At forty-four, Camus was the award's second-youngest recipient (Rudyard Kipling had won it at forty-two) and his enemies seized the opportunity to criticize him. Conservatives claimed that the Nobel committee was interfering in French internal affairs by giving the award to a known friend of the Algerian rebels. Paradoxically, the left generally condemned the choice because they felt Camus to be too withdrawn from the conflict, saying he had been cowardly in not choosing to support a side.

When Camus traveled to Stockholm in December to receive the award, he spoke to a group of students at Stockholm University. In the middle of his remarks he was interrupted by a young Arab who angrily accused him of supporting a repressive French colonial regime in Algeria. Camus replied that he had done what he could until he felt that his actions were only making the situation worse. He followed with an explanation of his ambivalent position that would often be quoted in years to come: "I must also denounce a terrorism which is exercised blindly, in the streets of Algiers for example, and which some day could strike my mother or my family. I believe in justice, but I shall defend my mother above justice."[11] He returned to Paris a few uneventful days later to continue his writing. He continued to work privately to ease the tensions in Algeria. For example, he sent petitions of clemency to French leader Charles de Gaulle on behalf of a number of Algerian Muslims. Publicly, he remained silent for fear of reprisals against his family.

Almost all of 1958 was devoted to finishing the adaptation of and beginning rehearsals for *The Possessed*, polishing the pieces for *Actuelles III* (published in late spring 1958) and writing *The First Man*. He and Francine purchased a house together in Lourmarin, a small town in Provence, and he spent a good deal of time tending to its restoration.

The Possessed opened in January 1958 and was met largely by indifference or shock at its nearly four-hour length. It closed after eight months without recovering its production costs, most of which had been provided by Camus and his associates. This led Camus to seek assistance from his friend Malraux, now a minister of culture in De Gaulle's cabinet. Malraux responded by supporting Camus's proposal to found a government-funded acting troupe. A meeting to finalize the plans for this group was scheduled for the week of Camus's untimely death.

Camus left Lourmarin on the morning of January 3, 1960, along with his friend Michel Gallimard and Gallimard's wife and daughter. They were driving the almost five hundred miles back to Paris after the New Year's holiday. In the early afternoon of the second day of their trip, Gallimard was at the wheel when their car went out of control near the small village of Villeblevin and smashed into a tree, killing Camus instantly and injuring Gallimard seriously (he died six days later). Camus's body was taken back to Lourmarin and buried on January 6.

Sartre, among others, eulogized Camus in print shortly after his death; although he did not rescind his criticism of eight years before, he did praise Camus as "the present-day heir of that long line of French moralists whose works constitute what is perhaps most original in French letters."[12] Camus's mother survived him by nine months and Francine Faure lived in the Lourmarin house for another nineteen years until her death in 1979.

A manuscript found in Camus's briefcase near the wreckage of Gallimard's car was subsequently edited by his daughter, Catherine, and published in 1994 as *The First Man.* Another unfinished novel, *A Happy Death,* was published in 1971.

NOTES

1. Patrick McCarthy, *Camus.* New York: Random House, 1982, p. 13.
2. Quoted in Herbert R. Lottman, *Albert Camus: A Biography.* Garden City, NY: Doubleday, 1979, p. 40.
3. Albert Camus, *Notebooks, 1935–1942.* New York: Knopf, 1963, p. 42.
4. Camus, *Notebooks, 1935–1942,* p. 143.
5. Camus, *Notebooks, 1935–1942,* pp. 172–73.
6. Lottmann, *Albert Camus,* p. 305.
7. Albert Camus, *Notebooks, 1942–1951.* New York: Knopf, 1965, pp. 96–97.
8. Lottmann, *Albert Camus,* p. 305.
9. Camus, *Notebooks, 1942–1951,* p. 228.
10. Lottmann, *Albert Camus,* pp. 586–87.
11. Quoted in Lottman, *Albert Camus,* p. 618.
12. Jean-Paul Sartre, "Tribute to Albert Camus" in Germaine Bree (ed.), *Camus: A Collection of Critical Essays.* Englewood Cliffs, NJ: Prentice-Hall, 1962, p. 173.

CHARACTERS AND PLOT

THE CHARACTERS

Very few characters in the novel are identified by their full names, so the "names" that appear here are the ones by which Meursault generally chooses to identify the various characters who appear in the book.

The Arab: Unnamed and only briefly described, he is the brother of a woman whom Raymond Sintès has physically abused. He and a companion follow Meursault and Raymond to the beach and physically confront them. He cuts Raymond with a knife and then flees. Later, Meursault finds him sitting on a rock and shoots him.

Marie Cardona: A former typist in Meursault's office. She becomes romantically involved with him on the day after his mother's funeral. She repeatedly asks Meursault if he loves her, to which he only replies that the question does not mean anything to him. She wants to marry Meursault but is somewhat discouraged by his lack of belief in the "seriousness" of marriage. When she testifies at his trial, she attempts to demonstrate that the prosecution's view of Meursault's actions in the wake of his mother's death are wrong, but she is largely ignored. She is the only one of his acquaintances who comes to visit Meursault once he is imprisoned, although she is only allowed to do so once, since they are not married.

Céleste: Owner of a restaurant at which Meursault regularly dines. He testifies at the trial that Meursault is both a regular customer and his friend. He attempts to convince the judge that Meursault's act was "just an accident" and clearly sympathizes with Meursault.

The Chaplain: A priest with whom Meursault has a heated conversation after his conviction. He insistently questions Meursault about his lack of belief in God and tries to make him admit that he feels guilt for his sin. When Meursault replies that he feels only an understandable fear of death, the priest states that he will pray to God to relieve Meursault's despair. Meursault finally loses his patience and roughly grasps the priest by the collar, screaming at him that guilt and death are meaningless concepts to him because they apply equally to all people. The jailers pull Meursault off the priest, who silently leaves the cell "with tears in his eyes."

The Doorkeeper: A sixty-four-year-old resident of the Home for Aged Persons who also serves in an official capacity as a doorman and jack-of-all-trades. He sits up with Meursault during the vigil the night before the funeral and talks at length about his youth in Paris and about the need to bury bodies quickly because of the heat. He later is called to testify at Meursault's trial about the fact that Meursault calmly drank coffee and smoked cigarettes during the vigil.

Emmanuel: Meursault's friend and coworker, with whom he regularly goes to lunch and from whom he borrows mourning clothes at the beginning of the novel.

The Employer: Meursault's boss, described by Meursault as somewhat reluctant to give him two days off for his mother's funeral. He offers Meursault a seemingly desirable job in Paris, but is dismayed by the lack of ambition that Meursault shows in turning it down. He criticizes Meursault for not wanting to "change his life" for the better.

The Examining Magistrate: Government official who interrogates Meursault after his arrest for the murder of the Arab. He asks Meursault to repeat his account of the shooting and wants to know why Meursault paused between firing the first shot and the remaining four. When Meursault does not answer, he shows Meursault a crucifix and speaks to him about repentance. He tells Meursault that all the criminals to whom he has previously shown the crucifix wept at the sight of it. Meursault becomes bored with the questioning and the interrogation ends.

The Lawyer: Apparently well meaning, but fairly incompetent, he is assigned to Meursault by the court after Meursault claims that he does not see the need for a lawyer. He counsels Meursault briefly on what he should expect during the trial, but then allows the Public Prosecutor to shift the focus of the trial away from Meursault's actions on the beach to his character in regard to his mother's death.

Masson: A friend of Raymond's who owns a bungalow on the beach. Raymond, Marie, and Meursault visit Masson and his wife on a Sunday morning, becoming fast friends and even beginning to plan for a month-long stay together at the house. After Masson comments to Meursault how "charming" Marie is, Meursault begins to think seriously about the possibility of marrying her. His testimony on Meursault's behalf at the trial is deemed irrelevant.

Meursault: His first name is never given in the novel, despite the fact that he is its main character. He works as a clerk in Algiers and lives a rather uneventful life in a small apartment in a middle-class district of that city. He had previously shared the apartment with his mother, but has lived alone since he placed her in the Home for Aged Persons. He is a quiet man who always measures his words carefully and does not speak unless he feels he has something to say. He becomes involved in a romantic relationship with Marie Cardona beginning on the day after his mother's funeral. He befriends his neighbor, Raymond Sintès, in part by helping him write a letter to an Arab woman that Raymond claims has been unfaithful to him. This letter leads to a violent confrontation between Raymond and the woman, and Meursault subsequently gives legal testimony that the woman had "let Raymond down." On the following Sunday morning, Meursault goes to the beach with Marie and Raymond to pass the day at the house of Masson, a friend of Raymond's. The brother of the woman Raymond had beaten follows them and a fight ensues on the beach in which Raymond is cut. Meursault returns to the beach afterwards, having previously taken Raymond's pistol away from him. He meets the Arab again and eventually shoots him, although the reasons for doing so are not entirely clear, either to Meursault or the reader. After a brief pause, he shoots the already lifeless Arab four more times. He is tried and convicted of murder and sentenced to be guillotined. As the book ends, he is awaiting the inevitable negative outcome of his appeal and attempting to come to terms with his imminent death.

"Mother" (Madame Meursault): Although she is dead at the start of the novel, her presence is felt throughout the book as a force that has influenced Meursault's character. She and Meursault shared an apartment for several years, although apparently without much interaction. She lived with him until he decided that he could no longer care for her and placed her in the Home for Aged Persons at Marengo, a two-hour bus ride from Algiers. Meursault states that she cried a great deal when she first arrived at the home

but gradually settled in there. During the last year of her life, he stopped going to visit her regularly, claiming that it would have disrupted her new life separate from him. She and Thomas Pérez became such close friends that the other residents jokingly claim that they are engaged.

Thomas Pérez: An elderly man who the warden claims had "become inseparable" from Meursault's mother before her death. He tearfully walks in her funeral procession, frequently taking short cuts to keep up, and then faints from exhaustion during the actual funeral service. He is called to testify at the trial as to whether Meursault wept at the funeral. He says "no" but his testimony is angrily challenged by Meursault's lawyer, causing Meursault to sympathize with the old man.

The Public Prosecutor: Because of the tactics he uses in attempting to convict Meursault, he is presented as a very unsympathetic symbol of public opinion. He constructs the majority of his case against Meursault on the premise that his lack of emotional response to his mother's death proves that he was "already a criminal at heart" even before shooting the Arab. At the height of his condemnation of Meursault, he goes so far as to claim that Meursault is guilty not only of the murder of the Arab but also guilty of the parricide in the case that follows.

The "Robot Woman": A woman who sits at Meursault's table during a meal at Céleste's restaurant. Meursault watches her as he eats, noting the mechanical way in which she adds up her bill in advance and makes notes in a listing of radio programs. He attempts to follow her after the meal, but her pace is too quick for him and he goes home instead. He notices that she is present at the trial and remarks several times that she is staring at him.

Salamano: Meursault's neighbor, an older man whose wife has died and who owns a mangy spaniel that he abuses, verbally and physically. Salamano draws the ire of most of the inhabitants of the apartment house because of his mistreatment of the dog, but Meursault remains ambivalent. When the dog disappears, Salamano comes to Meursault looking for comfort and advice. Meursault speaks with the old man but offers him only the reassurance that the pound keeps strays for three days. The next day, Salamano speaks with Meursault again about the dog, telling him how the dog has been his only companion since the death of his wife.

Meursault's only response is to tell him that the dog seemed well bred. Salamano tells Meursault that he does not believe the "nasty things" people have been saying about why he sent his mother away to the home. He testifies on Meursault's behalf at the trial, but is ignored.

Raymond Sintès: A neighbor of Meursault who claims to be a warehouseman but is reputed around the neighborhood to be a pimp. He invites Meursault to share his dinner one evening and tells him a lengthy and detailed story about some trouble he has had with a woman and her brother. He convinces Meursault to write a letter for him and almost immediately begins referring to him as his "pal." When the woman later shows up at his apartment, Raymond beats her so severely that a policeman is forced to intervene. He asks Meursault to testify on his behalf, which he agrees to do. When Raymond, Marie, and Meursault go to the beach to visit Masson and his wife, he meets the brother of the woman he has assaulted and is injured during a fight. A doctor treats his mild wounds, after which Raymond goes back to the beach with the intention of provoking the man into a further confrontation so that he can shoot him. Meursault takes his gun away from him and brings Raymond back to Masson's house. At Meursault's trial, Raymond tries to testify on behalf of Meursault, but the Prosecutor is interested only in showing that Meursault is befriending unsavory individuals such as Raymond.

The Warden: In charge of the nursing home and for the arrangements for the funeral of Meursault's mother. He speaks briefly with Meursault before the vigil about his mother's wish to be buried "with the rites of the Church," which comes as a surprise to Meursault. Later, he tells Meursault about the relationship between Thomas Pérez and his mother and accompanies him on the walk from the home to the church in Marengo. His testimony at the trial about Meursault's calmness during the funeral is central to the Prosecutor's goal of making Meursault seem heartless.

PLOT SUMMARY

Part I, Chapter One: Meursault receives a telegram informing him that his mother has died and that the funeral will be the next day, a Friday. He arranges for two days off from his job as a clerk in a firm, although this time is apparently given to him only grudgingly by his employer. He eats lunch at Céleste's restaurant and borrows a black tie and a mourner's armband from Emmanuel before catching the bus for Marengo, where the Home for Aged Persons is located.

On arriving at the home, he meets the doorkeeper, who tells him he must see the warden before he can see his mother's body. He waits briefly until the warden is free to see him and talks briefly with him about his mother's life in the home. The warden tells Meursault that his mother wished to have a church burial, which Meursault finds odd since he remembers his mother as having been uninterested in religion. The warden takes him to the mortuary where his mother's coffin has been placed, watched over by an Arab woman with a bandage on her face. The doorkeeper returns with a screwdriver to take the lid off the coffin. He is somewhat surprised when Meursault tells him that he does not wish to see his mother's body. The doorkeeper talks with Meursault about Paris and about the home's practices concerning funerals. The doorkeeper suggests some *café au lait* and they drink together. Afterward, Meursault smokes a cigarette, offering one to the doorkeeper as well.

At nightfall, ten of the other residents of the home arrive to take part in the all-night vigil over the coffin. Meursault remarks that he had the odd sensation that they were acting as his jury. Only one of the residents cries during the vigil and the doorkeeper explains that Meursault's mother had been her only friend in the home. Meursault falls asleep several times during the night. At daybreak on Friday morning, the residents depart, each shaking Meursault's hand on their way out. He has some more coffee and walks around the grounds of the home briefly before the warden asks to see him again. Meursault signs some forms and reiterates his lack of interest in seeing his mother's corpse before the funeral. The warden tells him that he and Meursault will be the only mourners at the funeral except for Thomas Pérez, an old man with whom Meursault's mother had become very close in the last years of her life.

The priest and the rest of the funeral procession arrive and they set out for the forty-five-minute walk to the church in Marengo. As they walk, Meursault notes that the day is getting unbearably hot and that Pérez repeatedly takes shortcuts to keep up with the procession. Meursault briefly talks with one of the undertaker's helpers, a conversation in which he fails to remember his mother's age. On arrival at the church, Pérez faints and Meursault admits to remembering very few details about the actual funeral. He catches a bus back to Algiers and delights in the thought of sleeping for twelve straight hours.

Chapter Two: Meursault wakes on Saturday morning and understands that part of his employer's hesitation at giving him two days off was that he would have a four-day weekend as a result. He spends the morning swimming, meeting Marie Cardona, a former typist from his office, at the pool. They flirt mildly at the pool and then decide to go to a comic movie featuring Fernandel that evening. Marie is momentarily surprised at Meursault's seeming indifference when he tells her that his mother's funeral had been the day before, but she goes to the movie anyway. Their flirtation becomes more physical during the film and they eventually return to Meursault's apartment, apparently to sleep together.

Marie departs early in the morning and Meursault remains in bed until noon. He observes that his apartment, which he formerly shared with his mother, has seemed too large for him since he placed her in the nursing home. He has moved all of his belongings—a dresser, a table, his bed, some rickety chairs, and a wardrobe—into the bedroom and leaves the rest of the apartment unused. He makes himself a breakfast out of what he has in the apartment and spends the remainder of the day in various trivial pursuits—pasting a newspaper clipping into a scrapbook, watching people go by from his balcony for long hours, smoking cigarettes, making himself a spaghetti dinner, and reflecting that very little has changed in his life despite the death of his mother.

Chapter Three: When Meursault returns to work on Monday, he finds that he has a great deal of work to catch up on. He and his friend from work Emmanuel run to catch up with a truck in order to get a ride to Céleste's for lunch. As is customary in Algeria, Meursault returns home for a nap after lunch, claiming to have had too much wine with his meal. When he gets back to work, he feels oppressed by the heat of the day. As he walks home, he feels pleased and calmed by the coolness of the evening. As he enters the hallway of his building, he passes his neighbor Salamano, who is taking his sickly old dog out for a walk. He remarks on the seeming state of hatred that exists between Salamano and his dog and notes that a number of people are appalled by the physical and verbal abuse that Salamano showers on his dog.

As he leaves Salamano, he is approached by Raymond Sintès, another neighbor, who invites him to share a dinner of black pudding and wine. Meursault agrees, saying that it will save him the trouble of cooking, and joins Raymond in his thoroughly disheveled apartment. Almost immediately, Raymond begins telling Meursault about a fight he got into that afternoon and the circumstances that led up to it. He relates a story of an Arab woman he had been involved with who he now claims was unfaithful to him despite his financial support. The fight he was involved in that day was with the woman's brother. Raymond is widely believed by the neighbors to be a pimp, but claims to be a warehouse worker. Raymond tells Meursault how he beat the woman after discovering her infidelity but also how he wishes for her to be somehow punished further. He asks Meursault to write a letter that will trick her into coming back to Raymond's apartment, at which point he plans to humiliate her further. Meursault agrees and in the process of writing the letter gains Raymond's almost immediate acceptance. They finish two bottles of wine and talk briefly about Meursault's mother before he returns to his own apartment and hears Salamano's dog through the wall moaning in the darkness.

Chapter Four: Meursault quickly skims through the details of a busy week at work, adding that Raymond stopped by once to say that he mailed the letter and that Meursault had gone to the movies twice with Emmanuel. Meursault and Marie go swimming in the ocean on Saturday morning, and frolic together happily in the water. They kiss and then return to his apartment and make love in the cool night air.

She spends the night in his apartment and as they are making plans for lunch on Sunday morning, they overhear Salamano screaming at his dog. Meursault explains the interaction between the old man and the dog to her and she laughs, which makes him note that he wanted to kiss her whenever she laughed. She asks him if he loves her and he replies that the question is meaningless to him.

As they are making lunch, they hear a woman shouting in Raymond's room and run out onto the landing. Raymond is apparently beating the woman severely, and Marie asks Meursault to get the police, which he refuses to do, claiming that he dislikes the police. A policeman brought by another neighbor pounds on Raymond's door. Raymond answers it insolently, a cigarette hanging from his mouth, which the policeman knocks away by hitting Raymond on the cheek. His insolence fades somewhat after this and the woman accuses him of being a pimp and of beating her. Raymond protests that she is slandering him in front of his neighbors. The policeman accuses Raymond of being drunk and asks him why he is trembling. He replies that he is not drunk and that it is natural to tremble while being questioned by a policeman. The policeman tells Raymond to stay in his room until summoned by the police and sends the woman away.

A few hours later, Raymond comes to Meursault's apartment and asks him if he had expected him to act differently with the policeman. Meursault claims he had not expected anything in particular and agrees to testify on Raymond's behalf that the woman had been unfaithful to him. Meursault and Raymond go out for a drink and to play billiards. Raymond suggests going to a brothel, but Meursault is not interested.

As they return to the apartment building, they meet Salamano, who is desperately searching for his dog. He fears that the police have taken his dog away, but Meursault tells him that the police have a pound where they keep all the animals that they find and that his dog is probably there. Salamano alternately rages that his dog is not worth the trouble of retrieving and frets that he will not be able to get him back. Meursault returns to his room and Salamano knocks on his door after a brief interval. He refuses to enter but wishes to be reassured that his dog will not be taken away. Meursault tells him that all animals are kept for at least three days, but Salamano is still fearful of being alone. Meursault hears the sound of what he believes to be Salamano weeping and thinks briefly of his mother. He notes that he has a busy day tomorrow and goes to bed without eating dinner.

Chapter Five: While at work, Meursault receives a phone call from Raymond inviting him to go to the beach on the following Sunday. Meursault tells him that he has a date with Marie planned for that day but Raymond insists that he bring her along. Raymond also tells Meursault that he has been followed through the streets by some Arabs, including the brother of the woman he has beaten. He asks Meursault to tell him if they are around when he returns home that evening.

Meursault hangs up and is called into his employer's office. Meursault fears that he is going to be reprimanded for talking on the telephone, but instead his employer offers him a job in Paris. When Meursault is noncommittal about the offer, his employer mildly chastises him for his lack of ambition in his work. As Meursault returns to his desk, he remarks that he was ambitious as a student, but ceased to be once he decided that ambition was useless.

Marie comes to his apartment that evening and asks him to marry her. He again displays an ambivalent attitude and she becomes upset with him, asking whether or not he loves her. He repeats his previous assertion that the question is meaningless and they disagree about what, if any, meaning there is in marriage. He agrees to marry her whenever she wishes and follows up by telling her about the job offer he received earlier in the day. He recounts his experience of having lived in Paris in his youth, saying only that it was "dingy" and that the women were generally attractive. He invites her to dinner, but she refuses, saying that she is busy. He does not ask what she is doing, which vexes her momentarily, but they part with a kiss.

Meursault goes to eat dinner at Céleste's and a strange woman shares the table with him. While she eats, she meticulously totals her bill and makes markings in a radio program guide. Meursault is slightly intrigued by her, calling her "my robot," and briefly follows her after dinner before tiring from keeping up with her rapid pace.

As he arrives home, he again meets Salamano, who despairs that his dog is certainly lost. Meursault invites him into his room where they sit and talk about the dog, the death of Salamano's wife, and the impropriety of the rumors circulating in the neighborhood about why Meursault sent his mother to the home. Salamano tells Meursault he doesn't believe these stories and Meursault reiterates his practical reasons for having acted the way he did. Salamano leaves wistfully and returns to his own apartment.

Chapter Six: Despite feeling lethargic and having a headache, Meursault awakens (with help from Marie) and prepares to go to the beach. His mood improves gradually as Marie and Raymond join him and they set out to catch the bus for the beach. Meursault mentions in passing that he successfully testified on Raymond's behalf the night before. While walking toward the bus, they see the Arabs whom Raymond had mentioned on the phone, but the Arabs do not seem particularly interested in accosting them. As they ride toward the beach, Meursault notices that Raymond continually tries to impress Marie. Meursault is pleased by the fact that she does not return his attention and smiles at Meursault instead.

They arrive and walk across a lengthy stretch of beach before getting to Masson's bungalow, where introductions are exchanged. Masson is a friend of Raymond's and he and his wife hospitably greet the others. Meursault sees Marie speaking with Masson's wife and seriously considers the possibility of marrying her. Masson suggests a swim and is joined by Marie and Meursault. Marie goes in the water immediately, while Masson and Meursault chat on the beach. Masson tells Meursault that Marie is "charming." They eventually join her in the water and swim for a while before returning to the house for a sizable lunch.

In the early afternoon, Raymond, Masson, and Meursault go for a walk on the beach. Meursault repeatedly mentions the heat and the brightness of the sun. During their walk, they cross paths with the Arabs from before. Raymond confronts the brother and a fight ensues during which Raymond is cut on the arm and mouth. Meursault does not take part in this confrontation and the Arabs eventually run off. Masson takes Raymond to a doctor to examine his injuries and Meursault returns to the house to explain what has happened to Marie and Masson's wife. When Masson and Raymond return, Raymond immediately wants to go for a walk on the beach. Despite his protestations, Meursault joins him and together they again encounter the Arabs, now unthreatening. Raymond grips his revolver and asks Meursault if he should shoot the Arabs. When Meursault responds that he should not shoot them unless they threaten him with the knife again, Raymond hands him the revolver. While this takes place, the Arabs run off and Raymond and Meursault go back to the house.

When they return to the house, Raymond goes inside, but Meursault claims that he is too hot to be "amiable to the women" so he walks back toward the rock where they had encountered the Arabs. He again notes the sweltering heat and the bright sunshine. When he gets to the rock, he is surprised to find the Arabs there. The Arab with whom Raymond had fought draws his knife and threatens Meursault with it. Meursault pulls out the revolver and shoots the Arab once. After brief reflection on what has happened, he shoots the Arab's prostrate body four more times.

Part II, Chapter One: Now imprisoned, Meursault undergoes a number of preliminary examinations about the murder of the Arab. Eventually, he is brought before the examining magistrate, who asks him if he has a lawyer. When Meursault replies that he does not, the magistrate tells him that the court will appoint one for him. Meursault feels congenial toward the magistrate and almost reaches to shake his hand as he leaves.

The next day, Meursault's lawyer comes to his cell to discuss the case. He tells him that the investigators have been looking into his behavior at his mother's funeral and that he has been described as showing "great callousness" there. Meursault tells the lawyer about his feelings toward his mother's death and asks the lawyer why this is relevant to the murder trial. The lawyer responds that this comment shows Meursault's inexperience with the law and counsels him on what he should and should not say at the trial.

Meursault meets with the magistrate again late that same day. The magistrate asks Meursault about his "self-centered" nature and Meursault responds that he speaks only when he feels he has something to say. The magistrate asks why Meursault fired five times in a row at the Arab, to which Meursault responds that he fired the final four shots after a momentary pause, although he cannot explain why.

The magistrate takes a crucifix out of a drawer and begins to discuss the nature of sin and repentance with Meursault, who is somewhat uninterested and has trouble seeing the connections the magistrate is trying to make with his situation. The magistrate asks Meursault if he believes in God and Meursault says that he does not, a position the magistrate finds impossible since in his view, "even those who reject Him" believe in God. He claims that Meursault's unbelief would make the magistrate's own life meaningless, which Meursault does not understand. When the magistrate tells Meursault that all other criminals to whom he has shown the crucifix have wept, Meursault nearly replies that this is precisely because they *were* criminals. He realizes, seemingly for the first time, that he too now falls into this category. The magistrate closes the interrogation by asking Meursault if he regrets his actions, to which Meursault replies that he feels not regret but a sort of "vexation."

The magistrate interviews Meursault on a number of subsequent occasions, in all of which Meursault's lawyer is present and speaks more than Meursault himself. Although the magistrate still seems affable toward Meursault, the remaining examinations pertain to purely legal matters, unlike the previous, more personal exchange.

Chapter Two: Meursault describes his initial experiences in the jail, from being put in a large cell with a number of other prisoners (mostly Arabs) to feelings of resignation at being imprisoned. He is eventually moved to a cell by himself, from which he is brought to see Marie when she makes the one visit she is allowed. They speak to each other, shouting across a thirty-foot divide in a room crowded with other prisoners and their visitors. Though he is glad to see her, his attention drifts toward some of the other conversations beside him.

When he returns to his cell he begins to become acclimated to life in prison. He has a conversation with the jailer in which he discusses the reasoning behind depriving him of cigarettes and women. The jailer explains that this is precisely the nature of punishment, taking away a prisoner's freedom to do what he wishes. He describes how he has learned to pass the time in prison by remembering minute details about his apartment. He also finds a newspaper article about a grisly murder in Czechoslovakia that he reads over and over to pass the time.

He spends an afternoon shining up his tin pan and looks at himself for a long time in it, remarking that he always has the "same mournful, tense expression." He watches the sun set and notices that he has been talking to himself for much of the day. As the chapter closes, he recalls a remark the nurse at his mother's funeral had made ("Now I'll leave you to yourself") and realizes that this applies to life in prison as well.

Chapter Three: Almost a year after his initial imprisonment, Meursault is brought to court to stand trial. His lawyer tells him that he expects the trial to be a quick one, since the case that follows is a complex parricide. He enters the courtroom and is surprised by the size and the composition of the crowd. A policeman explains to him that the press has generated a great deal of interest in his case, as is demonstrated by the number of journalists in attendance. A journalist tells Meursault that his case has been featured prominently because there are few other things to write about at the moment.

The trial begins and Meursault looks around the room and, again to his surprise, sees a number of familiar faces: Raymond, Masson, Salamano, the doorkeeper, Pérez, Marie, Céleste, and the woman with whom he had shared a table at Céleste's restaurant. The judge gives instructions to the crowd assembled to maintain order and then begins to question Meursault formally about the details of the crime. Meursault notices for the first of many instances that the "robot woman" and a particular journalist are staring at him intently. Meursault is antagonistically questioned by the Public Prosecutor about his motives and then the trial breaks for lunch.

After the break, Meursault notes that the courtroom is even hotter than before and that fans have been provided for everyone except himself. A series of witnesses testify, beginning with the warden, who reports that Meursault's mother complained about being placed in the home and that Meursault was very calm throughout his mother's funeral. The Prosecutor becomes sanctimonious after the doorkeeper testifies that Meursault drank coffee and smoked at the vigil. As a result, Meursault becomes uncomfortably aware that he is guilty in the eyes of the assembled crowd. When Pérez testifies that he was overcome with grief at the funeral the Prosecutor tries to call attention to the fact that Meursault, in contrast, did not even weep. Meursault's lawyer tries to contest this claim but is mostly ineffective. Céleste, Marie, Salamano and Raymond all attempt to testify for Meursault, but their words are either ignored or used against them by the Prosecutor to make Meursault seem terribly uncaring. Meursault's lawyer loses his patience again after the questioning of Raymond, asking whether Meursault is on trial for burying his mother or for murder. The Prosecutor replies that Meursault's behavior at the funeral demonstrates his general lack of feeling and proves that he was capable of the murder.

The court adjourns for the day and Meursault is returned to his cell, where he listens to the noises coming from outside. He remarks that this hour of evening had been his favorite time of day, but that he is unable now to enjoy it because of the prospects of a sleepless night.

Chapter Four: The next day of the trial is almost entirely taken up by the summary arguments made by the Prosecutor and by Meursault's lawyer. Meursault prefaces these by saying that "there wasn't any very great difference between the two speeches." The Prosecutor recounts Meursault's actions in the days after his mother's funeral and accuses Meursault of being wholly immoral and even of lacking a soul entirely. At the height of his rhetoric, the lawyer accuses

Meursault on the basis of his lack of morality of the death of his mother and even of the murder case being tried the next day. When asked for his response, Meursault only says that he had no intention of killing the Arab and that the sun had caused him to commit the crime. The audience is both puzzled and mildly amused by this statement. Meursault's lawyer asks for and receives an adjournment until the following day.

The speech given by Meursault's lawyer interests Meursault only in its rhetorical strategy. He awkwardly tries to counter the Prosecutor's claims about Meursault's lack of a soul, but in doing so fails to address a number of potential arguments directly related to the murder that could help Meursault's case. Meursault becomes bored and is eventually distracted by the noise of an ice-cream vendor outside the courtroom. His lawyer sums up his statement by saying Meursault will be duly punished by the lifetime of remorse that will follow and receives the stiff congratulations of some of his colleagues. Meursault realizes that he has not looked around the courtroom for Marie at any point during the trial and spots her. She responds with a nervous wave of the hand.

The judge sends the jury away with instructions to deliberate and Meursault discusses the prospects for the outcome of the case with his lawyer. His lawyer tells him that there is a good chance he will receive only a sentence of a few years, although he also informs him that there is no chance of getting the case thrown out entirely. Meursault waits for about an hour, at which point he is led back into the courtroom to hear the verdict. He notices that the journalist who stared at him throughout the trial is now looking away and hears the verdict decreeing his decapitation "in the name of the French people." He decides that the looks on the faces of those in the crowd are ones of sympathy for him and declines any statement in response to the verdict. He is led out of the courtroom.

Chapter Five: Meursault repeatedly refuses to speak with the chaplain. He ponders whether or not a "loophole" by which he can escape execution exists, finally deciding that it does not, since certainty is inherent in the very nature of the system that has decreed his execution. He ponders various aspects of the guillotine and describes his fear at the sound of footsteps at sunrise that would presage his execution. He

imagines both the potentially positive and negative out-
comes of his appeal.

During one such reverie, the chaplain enters the cell and
begins to talk to Meursault about repentance and God's forgiveness. Meursault again states that he does not believe in
God and adds that he does not despair because of what is
happening to him. Meursault says he only feels the understandable fear of one about to die but that the thought of God
does not offer him any solace since it is meaningless. Meursault gradually loses interest in the priest entirely but responds with increasing irritation to the priest's assertions
about Meursault's need to rid himself of guilt for his sins.
The priest mentions that other prisoners have told him that
they saw the face of God in the walls of the cell, but Meursault counters that the only face he had tried to see (unsuc-
cessfully, at that) was Marie's. The priest tells Meursault he
will pray for him, at which point Meursault takes the priest
roughly by the collar and begins shouting at him. Meursault
screams that all people are equally guilty and all equally
fated to die, conditions that make any comfort he could de-
rive from belief in God meaningless. The jailers enter, pull
Meursault away from the priest, and are about to hit him
when the priest stops them from doing so. He leaves the
room in tearful silence and Meursault, alone again, becomes
calm once more.

He sleeps briefly and awakens after nightfall. He remarks
on some of the peaceful sounds and smells of night coming
through his barred window and then comes to a realization
about his mother's relationship with Pérez. He resigns himself
to his fate and maintains that he is happy despite all that has
happened to him. As the book ends, Meursault expresses a desire to have a large and angry crowd witness his execution.

CHAPTER 1

Philosophical Themes in *The Stranger*

Indifference as the Guiding Principle of *The Stranger*

Alba Amoia

Alba Amoia, professor emeritus of Italian at Hunter College in New York, claims that the central message of the novel can be reduced to a simple three-word phrase: "it's not important." Amoia argues that Camus uses Meursault, a killer who essentially does not understand his own guilt, as part of a symbolic demonstration of the meaninglessness of the values that govern life in the pre-WWII world. According to Amoia, the indifference Meursault displays—even towards his own death—is evidence of Camus's lack of faith in concepts such as justice or perhaps even truth.

Algerian sunlight, for Albert Camus, is sometimes "so bright that it becomes black and white," and the countryside, at certain hours, glows "black with sun." Meursault, the protagonist of *The Stranger* (1942), before whose sun-dazzled eyes the parched earth and its vacillating forms coagulate in dark brilliance, commits a murder on a North African beach "because of the sun."

The symbolic novel unfolds in Algiers in the 1930s and narrates, in the simplest language, the story of a Frenchman who, in a fit of apparently inexplicable violence, psychologically and physically blinded by the African sun, kills an Arab—an Algerian Muslim—on a deserted beach. The name of the Frenchman is Meursault, an office clerk without ambition for advancement or success, without aspiration to a better life-style either through marriage, promotion, or transfer to a Paris office. Meursault appears perfectly content with his own existence, his own truths, his own trivial pleasures; he lives in his own private world, indifferent to the opinions of others, without regard for social mechanisms. After the crime, condemned to death on the guillotine, he accepts the verdict without reaction or emotion, without anger or contrition. He is a "stranger" among men, a murderer without guilt, condemned to die because a slight difference sets him apart from others.

Meursault relates his story in the first person, beginning with the bald statement: "Today, mother died. Or perhaps yesterday, I don't know." Whether Meursault's mother died today or yesterday is insignificant; whether the Arab's death was accidental or intentional is irrelevant; that Meursault's life will be cut short because he simply is uninterested in defending himself is inconsequential. "It's all the same to me"; "it's not my fault"; "it doesn't matter"—these are the phrases Meursault uses in reference to the events and vicissitudes of daily life. The principal leitmotiv throughout the novel is "it's not important." Nothing is important except what Meursault himself, in his aberrancy, considers meaningful: the pleasures of certain physical sensations; the rejection of sentimentality and social conformity; solitude; and the ultimate discovery that he can spurn the consolation of religion and the illusion of immortality, to take his place among those privileged "brothers" who have lived out their tragic destinies before him.

MEURSAULT'S LIFE AND CHARACTER BEFORE THE MURDER

In the opening scene of *The Stranger*, which is repeatedly recalled in other parts of the novel, Meursault has been notified of his mother's death and betakes himself to the geriatric home where the old lady has resided for several years. Deepening dusk pervades the little white room that serves as a morgue and where the pale corpse lies draped in black.

Instead of staying awake and keeping watch all night, as is customary and traditional even though purposeless, Meursault dozes fitfully while the other watchers sleep soundly, reinforcing his conviction that basically the dead woman was of no importance to any of them. Yet he will later be accounted monstrous for having slept through the vigil, for not having asked to have the coffin opened one last time to look at his mother, for not having shed a single tear, for not knowing his mother's age, for having left the cemetery immediately after the burial, without kneeling in prayer at the grave—trivial details that prove of infinite importance in helping the jury to decide that Meursault's life should not be spared.

After the funeral, Meursault's solitary life remains unchanged. He continues to devote himself to the usual banal activities and diversions of an obscure bachelor whose job fills his week and whose weekends are spent in the company of a girlfriend, Marie Cardona, a typist who used to be employed in his office. Marie would like Meursault to love her and marry her. He apathetically acquiesces to marriage—it's all the same to him—but admits honestly that he doesn't share Marie's feelings of love. A casual encounter with one of his neighbors will, however, soon change the course of his life. Raymond Sintès, a brutish-looking, ill-famed pimp, involves Meursault in his private dispute with an Arab mistress. At Raymond's request, Meursault composes and writes a letter inviting the young woman to a rendezvous at which she will be cruelly beaten. Again, as earlier in the story, Meursault hears his own blood pounding in his ears—a clear premonition of death. He nevertheless continues his association with Raymond and his friends, one of whom, Masson, invites him to bring Marie to spend a Sunday at his beach house on the outskirts of Algiers.

Outside their apartment house that Sunday morning, Raymond spots a group of Arabs, among them the brother of his ex-mistress, who has been trailing him ever since the affair of the beating. Later, two of the Arabs unexpectedly appear on the beach where Masson, Raymond, and Meursault are strolling under the dazzling noonday sun. Raymond, alert to the impending danger, assigns responsibilities in the event of a clash: he personally will take on his mistress's brother; Masson is to attack the companion; and, should a third Arab appear, Meursault is to assail him. A bloody battle ensues in which Raymond is stabbed in the arm and mouth, after which the Arabs flee.

Later in the day, Raymond, bandaged and armed with a revolver, returns to the beach under the crushing sunlight, Meursault following to keep an eye on him. They reach a freshwater spring hidden behind a huge rock where the two Arabs are reclining. The overexcited Raymond makes as if to shoot his adversary, but Meursault restrains him, pointing out that the Arab has said nothing nor has even drawn his knife. Meursault suggests that Raymond engage him rather in hand-to-hand combat and leave the gun to him in case the second Arab should intervene. But the Arabs, declining engagement, retreat behind the rock. Raymond and Meursault return to Masson's beach house, intending to take the next bus back to town.

At the moment of reentering the beach house, however, Meursault is seized by an inexplicable immobility, weariness, and apathy, accompanied by a feeling of intoxication and mental confusion. Eventually he turns around and retraces his steps along the beach, the veins of his forehead beating relentlessly under the skin. He longs to quench his thirst at the cool spring and bask in the shade of the rock, but when he reaches the spring, he again finds it "occupied" by Raymond's enemy. Meursault knows that he has only to turn around in order to avoid a confrontation, but, behind him, the beach, vibrating under the scorching, pitiless sun, seems to block his retreat and goads him on towards the spring. Meursault takes a step forward; the Arab draws his knife. The blinding sun, the sea, and the salty perspiration from his own brow drop a veil over Meursault's eyes; he becomes disoriented in time and space. His finger involuntarily pulls the trigger of Raymond's revolver, hesitates, then pumps four more bullets into the inert body on the ground.

MEURSAULT'S INTERROGATION, TRIAL, AND PUNISHMENT

Under interrogation by the prosecuting attorney and by the court-appointed lawyer assigned to defend him, Meursault (who would prefer to do without a lawyer) is unable to explain away the facts adduced by way of demonstrating his insensitivity. He honestly was unable to mourn the death of his mother. He knows that he did not return to the spring with the intention of killing the Arab, yet he honestly does not know why he did return, armed, to that particular spot, nor why he hesitated after the first shot, nor why he continued shooting once the body had fallen to the ground. He honestly does not believe in God, nor can he later repent in order to be pardoned; and though he is not hard-hearted, he is honestly unable to shed tears before the image of the crucified Christ that is offered by the prison chaplain. Whatever specious arguments his lawyer suggests by way of extenuation are vehemently rejected by Meursault, who becomes a martyr to strict truth. He does not attempt to justify himself in the eyes of his own lawyer, for he sees the futility of his own words; and though he would like to gain the lawyer's sympathy, he is too lethargic to seek it.

Gradually, as he awaits the leisurely course of justice, Meursault's thoughts change from those of a free man to those of a prisoner, keenly aware of the alternation of day and night. His little cell, with its high window against which he strains to view the light and the sea, becomes familiar, desirable. When Marie comes to visit him, he concentrates his hopes on the delicate fabric that covers her shoulders, which he yearns to grasp but from which he is separated by ten meters of space and two gratings that hold visitors and prisoners apart.

Up to the moment of the trial, Meursault feels no sense of guilt. It is only when the attendant of the geriatric home testifies that the accused did not take a last look at his mother and that he had smoked, slept, and drunk coffee in the presence of the corpse, that the indignation in the courtroom makes itself felt and, ironically, for the first time, enables Meursault to understand that he is guilty. His strict honesty in answering the questions put to him by his examiners has effectively worked against him; he now admits to the desire to weep, so conscious is he of the reprobation he has himself aroused. To this desire is counterpoised the scornful laughter in the courtroom at his truthful answer that he did not willfully intend to kill the Arab, that he killed "because of the sun." His simplicity and his innocence are so obvious that they can only result in a verdict of "guilty."

As the trial proceeds, the questioning and haranguing of his lawyer and the prosecuting attorney seem to reduce Meursault himself to a nonentity. They substitute themselves for him so completely that the central character begins to feel himself outside the entire affair and gains the impression that his destiny is being decided without even involving his own person. (In this respect, the British title of the novel, *The Outsider,* is especially appropriate.) Gradually, the suffocating heat in the courtroom and the interminable flow of words—evocative of the heat and prayers at his mother's burial, and premonitory of his own—together with the endless interrogations and the muddled concepts of a trial in which "everything is true and nothing is true," induce the same feelings of mental confusion and dizziness that had affected Meursault on the beach. Once the verdict of guilty is pronounced, Meursault vents his wrath against the prison chaplain, and at last finds peace and refreshment in the perfumes of the night and the earth, the salt sea air that fills his cell, cooling his burning, beating temples. The hated Meursault must die under the blade of the guillotine. The leitmotiv is again heard: it's not important how or when; he is as indifferent to his fate while still alive as he will be when dead. He opens his soul to the tender indifference of mankind in a world devoid of God, recognizes that he has known happiness through the sheer act of living, and hopes only that, in order to be less alone at his execution, there will be many spectators to greet him with cries of derision, so that he may fully live out his role in life and that his fate may be confirmed by a senseless manifestation of hatred.

Although it appeared in wartime, it is important to remember that *The Stranger* is a work of the prewar years and had been completed before the sudden German attack and collapse of French resistance in the spring of 1940. Its somber, sometimes paradoxical tone is the fruit of Camus's youthful ponderings, his rebellious disgust with the complacency and fraudulence of prewar society, but in no sense a reflection of the deeper, more universal tragedies in the midst of which it came before the public.

DEATH IN THREE VARIETIES

Three forms of death underpin the story of *The Stranger:* the natural death of an old woman; the homicide of a faceless Arab; and society's irreversible punishment of a basically honest and potentially salvageable criminal. Camus presents each of the three forms both realistically and symbolically, and links all three by means of sharp, smiting images of awful finality.

His dead mother is a victim of that killing force that is old age, which renders men and women feeble and helpless, then strikes to snatch away the very breath of life. No son or daughter, but death alone, is guilty of this crime. Yet an inevitable sense of guilt—although "it's not his fault"—stirs in the son who has been summoned to mourn, and the elements focused on in the mother's funeral scene convey both the bewilderment and the blindness surrounding death. The unexpected switching on of the dazzling electric lights in the morgue momentarily blinds Meursault. This premonitory scene is immediately followed by a description of Meursault himself, scarcely the bereaved son one would expect to meet, seated beside the bier and drinking coffee and smoking. He has, it is true, hesitated before lighting his cigarette, unsure whether it would be appropriate in the presence of the corpse—a hesitation that will be replicated in the pause between the first shot he fired at the Arab and the subsequent four. The accomplishment of both acts, after the moment of indecision, probably bespeaks Meursault's mental conclusion that "it doesn't matter"—a standpoint that precludes contrition and that, in the eyes of the jury that will condemn him, establishes his guilt. Twice will the attendant be called upon in court to tell the story of Meursault's coffee and cigarette; twice will Meursault be asked why he waited between the first and second shots—only to impress the jury, by his answers, with his guilt and thus to justify its capital verdict.

Even before the court scene in *The Stranger,* Camus had given the reader a foretaste of Meursault under judgment, in a description bringing Shakespeare's immortal lines [from *Measure for Measure*] to mind:

> The jury, passing on the prisoner's life,
> May in the sworn twelve have a thief or two
> Guiltier than him they try.

As the elderly inmates of the geriatric home file silently into the morgue to take their seats opposite Meursault and the corpse—and they are now twelve in the room—he sees them momentarily, in a kind of premonition, as sitting in judgment on him. He is unable to see their eyes "set in a nest of wrinkles" (again, symbolic blindness), and their toothless mouths move in incomprehensible murmuring sounds, perhaps an anticipation of the gentle sounds of the sea and the gurgling of the freshwater spring in the murder scene, or of the interminable flow of words during the court trial.

The funeral procession and burial ceremony take place in midmorning when the hot sun, the main symbol in the novel, already weighs heavily on the little cortege of mourners—a heaviness later to be mirrored in the murder scene, when the unbearable burning sun, in Meursault's mind, will be "the same . . . as the day I buried my mother." The priest who has been summoned to conduct the funeral calls Meursault "my son." Similarly, in the closing pages of the novel, another priest, the prison chaplain, will call Meursault "my son," provoking thereby a burst of nervous anger on the part of the condemned criminal, who refuses to accept identification with this "father" who represents for him a set of arbitrary beliefs shorn of any reality in this life.

At the close of the funeral scene, the reader is struck by certain images that presage the second death in *The Stranger:* the figure of one of the mourners whose blood-red ears stand out under his black hat; blood-red geraniums growing on the graves in the cemetery; the red earth being shoveled over the coffin of the dead woman; and Meursault's blood, which he hears pounding against his temples—a phenomenon that is frequently invoked by Camus at moments of high tension in his fictional works.

On the morning of the homicide of the faceless Arab, Meursault is once again "struck in the face" by the strong sunlight, just as his face had been flailed by the brightness of the light that flooded the morgue. On the beach, at the appearance of the Arab, Meursault notes that the overheated sand now looks red to him—a premonition of the bloodshed to come—and when Raymond later relinquishes his revolver to Meursault, the latter notices that liquid sun (blood) "spilled over it." Just prior to committing the crime, Meursault feels his head bursting from the "stabs" of sunlight that rise from the "red" sands. The Arab's knife gleams in the sun like a long, fiery sword pointed at the forehead of Meursault, who confuses the piercing pain of the sun with the sharp blade of the knife. Not Meursault, but the sun alone, is guilty of this crime that Meursault seems to have committed in self-defense.

These beach images lead directly to their capital verdict counterpart—the guillotine. Meursault's head will be severed from his body in the name of the French people. Are the French people, then, not guilty of legalized, rationalized murder, "guiltier than him they try?" The knowledge that the jury wills his death deters Meursault from any form of reconciliation or repentance, since it empties of meaning all conventionalities, including respectful burial of a mother or returning the love of a Maria Cardona.

The Stranger illustrates the deep internal contradictions within society's conventional attitudes, as well as the typical existentialist themes of the emptiness of the universe and the absurdity of human existence. Meursault, a lonely but, one must imagine, clear-sighted man, gives meaning to his life through his personal attitude and private experience. Like Meursault, Camus appears to be saying, contemporary man feels himself to be in an absurd situation because, even while he seeks value and justification for his existence, he discovers that society and events defeat his purpose. His subjective will would like to aspire to a rational universe and a life that takes men into account, but objective realities impel him in the opposite direction. Unable to accept a reality that is so blind to human aspirations, contemporary man falls victim to an "absurd" malaise. Indifferent, a stranger to himself, like Meursault, he can in the extreme case even allow himself to be condemned to death through sheer apathy.

Camus's message, delivered in a unique, sober, black-and-white style, was received by Jean-Paul Sartre with these words:

> The turn of his reasoning, the clarity of his ideas, the cut of his expository style and a certain kind of solar, ceremonious, and sad sombreness, all indicate a classic temperament, a man of the Mediterranean.

In a deeper sense, however, the significance of Meursault's experience for people situated in other times and in other places is something each reader must determine from an individual perspective.

Is Meursault a Stranger to the Truth?

Robert C. Solomon

In the preface to an early French edition of *The Stranger*, Camus asserts his belief that Meursault is incapable of telling a lie. Robert C. Solomon, professor of philosophy at the University of Texas at Austin, explicitly challenges this pronouncement, as well as similar ones made by subsequent critics. Solomon bases his contention largely on analysis of the difference between Meursault's narration before and after the murder of the Arab. He claims that Meursault should not be judged according to normal standards of truth and falsehood because he exists in a state of stunted psychological development at the beginning of the novel. Only after the shooting does he begin to be capable of reflecting on his actions instead of just experiencing the world around him, but this change comes too late to give his death any true meaning.

What would it be—not to lie? Perhaps it is impossible. It is not difficult to avoid uttering falsehoods, of course. One can always keep silent. But what if lying is also not *seeing* the truth? For instance, not seeing the truth about oneself even in the name of "not lying"? What then would it be not to lie?— to see oneself and one's feelings as brute facts, as matters already fixed and settled? The very idea of not lying would then be a lie.

The lie—the very heart of French Existentialism. It is the infamy of the human condition for Sartre, the gravest sin for Camus. But where Sartre suspects that the lie—or what he calls *mauvaise foi* [bad faith]—is inescapable, Camus glorifies his characters—and apparently himself—as men without a lie. Meursault of *The Stranger*, Camus tells us in a retrospective interpretation, "refuses to lie . . . accepts death for

Excerpted from "L'Etranger and the Truth," by Robert C. Solomon, *Philosophy and Literature*, Fall 1978. Copyright © 1978 by The Johns Hopkins University Press. Reprinted with permission from The Johns Hopkins University Press.

the sake of truth." Dr. Rieux of *The Plague* refuses to release information to Tarrou the reporter unless he reports "without qualification." Clamence of *The Fall* has been living a lie. He is now in purgatory (the seedy inner circles of Amsterdam), a judge-penitent: a judge, we come to see, of other people's hidden falsehoods, a penitent for his own past lie of a life. In *The Myth of Sisyphus,* it is "the absurd" that becomes the as-certainable truth, and it is the absurd hero who "keeps the absurd alive" with his defiant recognition of that truth. In the turmoil of French leftist politics through the Algerian crises and the Stalin show trials, Camus portrays himself in his *Journals* and in *The Rebel as* the "independent intellectual," the spokesman for the truth who refuses to accept the neces-sary political fabrications of the left during a time of crisis and change. Accordingly, Camus has himself been inter-preted and praised as the hero and martyr for the truth, as "Saint Just," the absurd hero and existential champion.

The Stranger is the best known of Camus's works, and it is on the basis of this early short novel that the interpreta-tions of Camus's philosophy reasonably begin. But virtually every interpretation of this work has resulted in what I shall argue to be a false claim—that Meursault is a totally honest man, the "stranger" who does not lie. In his own interpreta-tion of *The Stranger,* Camus writes,

> . . . the hero of the book is condemned because he doesn't play the game. In this sense he is a stranger to the society in which he lives; he drifts in the margin, in the suburb of pri-vate, solitary, sensual life. This is why some readers are tempted to consider him as a waif. You will have a more pre-cise idea of this character, or one at all events in closer con-formity with the intentions of the author, if you ask yourself in what way Meursault doesn't play the game. The answer is simple: He refuses to lie. Lying is not only saying what is not true. It is also and especially saying more than is true and, as far as the human heart is concerned, saying more than one feels. This is what we all do every day to simplify life. Meur-sault, despite appearances, does not wish to simplify life. He says what is true. He refuses to disguise his feelings and im-mediately society feels threatened. He is asked, for example, to say that he regrets his crime according to the ritual for-mula. He replies that he feels about it more annoyance than real regret and this shade of meaning condemns him.

> Meursault for me is then not a waif, but a man who is poor and naked, in love with the sun which leaves no shadows. Far from it being true that he lacks all sensibility, a deep tena-cious passion animates him, a passion for the absolute and

> for truth. It is a still negative truth, the truth of being and of feeling, but one without which no victory over oneself and over the world will ever be possible.

> You would not be far wrong then in reading *The Stranger* as a story of a man who, without any heroics, accepts death for the sake of truth. I have sometimes said, and always para-doxically, that I have tried to portray in this character the only Christ we deserved. You will understand after these explana-tions that I said this without any intention of blasphemy and only with the slightly ironic affection which an artist has the right to feel towards the characters whom he has created.

And throughout the standard interpretations, the same theme is unquestioningly repeated, e.g. ". . . this indifferent man is intractable in his absolute respect for truth," and "his principal characteristic appears to be a kind of total sincer-ity which disconcerts us because it is virtually unknown in our world."

. . . But I want to argue that this standard interpretation in all its forms is unconvincing, not just in detail, but in essence, and in spite of the fact that the author has endorsed it himself. I want to argue that the whole question of Meursault's "hon-esty" and "the lie" should be replaced by an examination of the presuppositions of honesty and a new kind of thinking about "feelings." For I want to argue that the character of Meursault is not to be found in the reflective realm of truth and falsity but exclusively in the prereflective realm of simple "seeing" and "lived experience." On the basis of certain phe-nomenological theories which were circulating around Paris in the 1940s and with which Camus was surely familiar, I want to argue that Meursault neither lies nor tells the truth, because he never reaches that (meta-)level of consciousness where truth and falsity can be articulated. Moreover, he does not even have the feelings, much less feelings about his feel-ings, to which he is supposed to be so true.

THE DEVELOPMENT OF MEURSAULT'S CONSCIOUSNESS

If *The Stranger* has so often been defended as a celebration of pure and honest feelings, it has also been said that Meur-sault is "strange" because he has no feelings. This is cer-tainly not true. He enjoys the warmth of the sun and Marie's company. He can be annoyed—by the sun or the fact that it's Sunday. But he does not feel regret for his crime nor sorrow for his mother's death. He is confused when Marie asks him if he loves her, not because he is undecided, but because he does not understand the question. What Meursault does not do is make judgments. As the narrator of the novel he describes, but he does not judge, the significance of his actions or the meaning of events, other people's feelings or his own. Accordingly, he does not reflect; he has few thoughts and is only minimally self-conscious. He cannot be true to his feelings, not only because he does not know what they are, but because, without judgments, he cannot even have them. His "true feelings," the feelings he actually has, are an emotionally emasculated and crippled portrait of human experience.

For those who construe Meursault as hero for the truth, his simple world of feelings must be treated as wholly autonomous, independent of reflection; his honesty is precisely the fact that he does not claim to be feeling anything more than what he actually feels. It is, in other words, as if the feelings were simply given and reflection merely commentary, a set of judgments *about* our feelings, with which we, according to Camus, "simplify" and thereby lie about life.

. . . To state my interpretation baldly, Meursault is a philosophically fantastic character who, for the first part of the novel, is an ideal Sartrian pre-reflective consciousness, pure experience without reflection, always other than, but also *nothing* other than what he is conscious of at the moment. He is a demonstration, even despite the author's intentions, of the poverty of consciousness, for it is only with judgments and reflection that the feelings we consider most human are possible. But then, in the second part of the novel, prison deprives him of his rich fund of totally involving Mediterranean experiences; his trial robs him of his indifference to others' opinions of him, thereby forcing him to reflect on himself and providing him with such emotions as regret, guilt and anger; the threat of imminent death finally forces him into a Heideggerian celebration of the "privilege of death" and the "happy death" which is a constant theme in Camus's novels (the last line of *The Plague*, the title of *La Mort Heureuse*) but a clumsy paradox in his philosophical essays. In Part II, Meursault begins to become a person, because he is condemned.

. . . In the first part of the book, Meursault does not reflect; he rarely speaks at all. He does not think. Those sporadic occurrences where a thought does appear to him, like a weed that has surprisingly pushed its way through the concrete, only illustrate how unthinking he is; e.g., "For some reason,

I don't know what, I began thinking of mother" and ". . . just in time, I remembered I killed a man." This is not thinking, certainly not reflecting. It is at most simply "having thoughts."

A problem: who is the narrator of Part I? It cannot consistently be the same Meursault who is unreflectively experiencing. It must be another Meursault, a reflective Meursault, other than the experiences to which he has special access. . . . It is this second Meursault who is the narrator, a necessarily reflective but not at all imaginative or philosophical reporter. But notice that the report is not contemporaneous with the experience: even though the novel begins in the brutal present ("Aujourd'hui, Maman est morte" ["Mother died today"]), it very soon (second paragraph) changes to the French present perfect tense and remains there. While the experiences are in ordinary temporal sequence, the reporting is not. On page 13, the narrator says, "But now I suspect that I was mistaken about this," and on page 70, "but probably I was mistaken about this." When is this *now?* It can only be in the time interval of Part II of the novel, in prison but (obviously) before the execution. On page 95 (in prison) the narrator reports, "it was *then* that the things I've never liked to talk about began."

If *The Stranger* were written from a third-person standpoint, Meursault would certainly not seem "strange," but he would have no character at all. It is from the first-person standpoint that Camus allows the Kantian or Husserlian Ego to report on the utter blandness of Meursault's prereflective consciousness as it matter-of-factly describes his world. Now, going back to Camus's warning, "lying is not only saying what is not true. It is also saying and especially saying more than is true," neither applies to the prereflective Meursault, who does not say enough to lie. But what of the reflective narrator? What is "true" for him would appear to be the flat, uninterpreted reporting of prereflective Meursault's experience, without addition or comment. But here we suspect that the entire first part of the book—however brilliant and sensitive—is a lie, for there can be no description of experience without some conceptualization, interpretation, and unavoidable, if minimal, commentary. Meursault of Part I is an impossible character because he is both the reflective transcendental narrator and the unreflective bearer of experience.

. . . Meursault is neither a hero nor an "anti-hero." He is more like the space from which the reader watches a world discover itself. It is a simple world, without interpretation and without personality. Meursault is Sartre's nothingness of consciousness, John Barth's Jacob Horner, but unlike Sartre or Horner, Meursault does not see himself as nothing, he simply is nothing; he does not see himself as anything at all. (It is impossible to be unhumorously grammatical in these matters.) Meursault might be described by others as "the man who . . . ," but he himself has no self-image until his trial, when he is for the first time forced to see himself as the "criminal": "I too came under that description. Somehow it was an idea to which I could never get reconciled.". . . He is learning what it is to apply ascriptions to himself, to "see himself in a social context." Early in the novel, in his flat, he says "I glanced at the mirror and saw reflected in it the corner of my table . . . "; like a vampire, *he* has no reflection, for reflections do not precede but are consequent upon concern with self-image. In prison, self-image becomes almost an obsession: he polishes his food tin to make a mirror, studies his face and his expression, does the same again later and critically reflects upon his "seriousness." Once, he hears his own voice, talking to himself.

MEURSAULT AND LACK OF EXISTENCE

It is not as if Meursault has been deprived by his author of a single superfluous dimension of human existence. He has been deprived of *human* existence altogether. On this point, the pompous prosecutor is right, even if his overloaded references to Meursault's "shameful orgies" (i.e., sleeping with Marie and watching a Fernandel film) and Meursault's virtual guilt for the parricide (his lack of visible mourning for his mother) easily lead us to dismiss everything he says. The prosecutor looked into Meursault's "soul," and "found a blank, literally nothing . . . ," "nothing human," "not one of those moral qualities" and "devoid of the least spark of human feeling."

Meursault the character is a piece of flat, colorless glass, allowing us to sense the warmth of the sun and smell the brine on the pillow, to crave a cigarette or a cup of coffee or conjure up a vision of thin-haired, hunched-up, skin-blotched Salamano dragging his mule-like mangy dog. We feel the flash of light reflected from the blade of a knife "sear our eyelashes and gouge our eyeballs," spot a "black speck on the sea that might be a ship," but we get no feeling for the *significance* of anything, not even enjoyment or disgust or fear. And it is judgments of significance that make most feelings possible. Meursault has no expectations, no desires other than immediate needs and urges, no sense of responsibility so no sense of guilt or regret, no ability to make moral judgments—and so feels neither disgust nor alarm at the sight of cruelty or danger. He has no conception of either commitment or fidelity, so such notions as love, marriage, and honesty have no meaning to him. He has no ambition, no dissatisfactions. (Even in prison he says, "I have everything I want.") He can feel vexation—an immediate feeling of malcontent and resentment, but not regret, which requires a view of oneself and the past for which one is responsible. He can feel desire but not love; he feels fondness for his mother but not grief; he has thoughts but does not think; he exists but does not think of himself as existing as anything.

. . . It has always seemed curious to me that the standard interpretation of Meursault as a man faithful to his feelings should persist in the face of the embarrassing fact that, throughout Part I of the novel, Meursault never has any significant feelings, even where it seems obvious *to us* that he *ought* to feel something. There are blanks and gaps in the narration where feelings ought to be in exactly the same way that there is an abyss where Meursault's "soul" ought to be. He is not disgusted by Salamano's treatment of his dog nor by Raymond's cruelty to the Arab woman; he is not frightened by the knife-wielding Arab nor moved by his mother's death nor by Marie, for whom his only "passion" appears to be the immediacy of sexual desire. Although there is at least one instance of shared enjoyment, Meursault typically treats Marie as a source of sensations. Any hint of personality on her part appears to Meursault merely as a stimulus. ("When she laughs I always want to kiss her.") He shows no sign of jealousy when he sees Raymond flirting with her, and he is at most "curious" when Marie "has other plans for the evening." He never thinks of Marie when she is not with him, until he is in prison, that is, when his thoughts are rather aimed at "some woman or other," but even those primitive sexual desires are apparently satisfied by his "doing like the others."

In a rightfully famous and startling passage, Marie asks
Meursault if he loves her. "I said that sort of question had no
meaning, really: but I supposed I didn't." Exactly the same
question and answer appear a few pages later. (It is not clear
whether the second phrase occurs in the conversation,
whether it is a reflective commentary or a thought occurring
to Meursault at the time.) When Raymond asks Meursault if
he would like to be "pals," he responds with similar indifference. With love and friendship, as with his mother's
death, "nothing in my life has changed." One would not expect Meursault to be an interesting lover, but we can see that
he could not be a lover at all. It is not a matter of his not loving Marie in particular nor a question of his not "saying
more than is true." Meursault has no *concept* of love (or
friendship or family). If "love" would mean anything to him,
it would have to be a sensation, something like the pleasure
he feels from the warmth of Marie's body or the smell she
leaves behind her. But love, as Camus must have been
aware—if not from Sartre at least from his early idol André
Gide—is not simply a feeling, but a system of judgments,
meanings, expectations, intentions, regrets, reflections.,
fears, obsessions, needs, and desires, abstract demands and
metaphysical longings. Of course there may also be pleasur-
able sensuous contact and feelings of animal warmth and
comfort, but these are—however desirable—less essential
than the more judgmental components of love, involving a
conception of oneself and another which Meursault does not
have.

In [his 1942 book] *The Myth of Sisyphus,* Camus comments, "But of love I know only that mixture of desire, af-
fection, and intelligence that binds me to this or that creature. That compound is not the same for another person. I do
not have the right to cover all these experiences with the
same name." But Camus the philosopher here makes the
same error that he builds into his unreflective creation; love
is not simply an experience nor a set of experiences, however complex. It has a necessary dimension which one
might call "commitment," not in any legal or moral sense,
but in that series of demands, memories, intentions, expectations, and abstractions which add up to a relationship
which cannot be simply "for the moment." ("Will you love
me forever, even if just for this weekend?") Meursault, who
understands only his sensuous feelings, can have no concept

of love, which is not a sensuous feeling; nor can he understand friendship or the abstract love of a son for his distant mother.

Since Meursault has no sense of commitment, we would expect that he must have an equally uncomprehending view of love's institutional variant (or fossilization) marriage:

> Marie came that evening and asked me if I'd marry her. I said I didn't mind; if she was keen on it, we'd get married. . . . I explained that it had no importance really, but if it would give her pleasure, we could get married right away. I pointed out that, anyhow, the suggestion came from her; as for me, I'd merely said, "Yes." Then she remarked that marriage was a serious matter. To which I answered, "No." She kept silent after that, staring at me in a curious way. Then she wondered whether she loved me or not. I, of course, couldn't enlighten her on that.

For Meursault (and, one sometimes suspects, for Camus), only spontaneous experience ("life") is meaningful. Ironically, Meursault, who has only such experiences, can find no meaning in his experience. He cannot know love or friendship, nor grief for his mother or regret for his crime. He is, as he tells us later, "too absorbed in the present or immediate future." He has no expectations, and consequently no fears or disappointments. In short, he has no feelings of consequence.

. . . One might hypothesize, in good philosophical tradition, that Meursault could not possibly sense feelings in others if he cannot comprehend them in himself. Quite right, but the logic of the argument—at least since Wittgenstein and Sartre—might better be reversed: it is only with an understanding of feelings in others that one can have an apprehension of one's own feelings. And if understanding feelings is a necessary condition for having feelings, one can argue that, unless one apprehends feelings in others, one cannot *have* them oneself. And so for Meursault. His "indifference" to other people and his indifference in general are two aspects of the same impossible opacity—his inability to interpret, his unwillingness to judge, to "say more than he feels."

Accordingly, people do not exist for Meursault. He only "observes" other people, as he once claims some Arabs viewed him, "like blocks of stone or dead trees," not without interest, but without compassion. At the vigil for his mother, Meursault watches the old people soundlessly usher them-

selves around the coffin: "Never in my life had I seen any-
one so clearly as I saw these people; not a detail of their
clothes or features escaped me. And yet I couldn't hear them,
and it was hard to believe they really existed." "For a moment I had the absurd impression that they had come to sit
in judgment of me." They are all "details of clothes and features." So of course it is "absurd" to think that they can judge
him. He sees that the old people cry, but he does not see
them grieve. He sees Marie pout at his responses to her, but
he does not see that she is hurt. He hears Raymond's girlfriend scream, but he does not see her pain. He sees Raymond bleed, but he does not see his pain or his anger. The
Arab Meursault shoots evidently feels or expresses nothing
whatever. They are all "little robots," like the woman seated
opposite him in Celeste's restaurant.

SELF-AWARENESS AS A KIND OF SALVATION

The movement from Part I to Part II of *The Stranger* is a
movement from innocence to awareness, but not only in the
"Christian" sense which has so often been pointed out. It is
a movement from pure unreflective experience to reflection
and philosophy. It is the second part of the book that carries
us into *The Myth of Sisyphus*. It is not in prereflective "indifference" or "honesty," but in his reflections before death that
Meursault becomes a model of the absurd hero, like Sisyphus, whose tragedy and whose salvation lies in the fact that
he is "conscious."

In the early stages of the indictment and interrogation,
Meursault regards his case as "quite simple." He is just beginning to characterize himself, to give himself an "essence"
on the basis of his past, as Sartre would say. It is not his case
but his reflections that are still "simple." As he learns to reflect on himself, his actions and his past, he loses his former
spontaneity, for example at the prosecutor's office: "When
leaving, I very nearly held out my hand and said 'Goodby':
just in time I remembered that I'd killed a man."

In Part I, Meursault invisibly observes the little "robot
woman" in the restaurant; in Part II, at the trial, he notices
only that she is *looking* at him. To reflect is to "see yourself,"
and to "see yourself" is to make yourself vulnerable to the
look of others. In court, Meursault learns of the existence of
other people, not as "details of features and clothing" but as
his *judges:* "It was then that I noticed a row of faces opposite

me. These people were staring hard at me, and I guessed they were the jury. But somehow I didn't see them as individuals. I felt as you do just after boarding a streetcar; and you're conscious of all the people on the opposite seat staring at you in the hope of finding something in your appearance to amuse them." Meursault develops an Ego, a bit of French vanity. At first he is delighted at the attention he is receiving. Later he feels left out of the camaraderie of the courtroom, "de trop" ["too much"], "a gate crasher," "excluded." But finally, the looks take their effect: the prosecutor's "tone and the look of triumph on his face, as he glanced at me, were so marked that I felt as I hadn't felt in ages. I had a foolish desire to burst into tears. For the first time, I'd realized how all these people loathed me;" and then, ". . . For the first time I understood that I was guilty."

"Guilt" here is not a premonition of the verdict, any more than the desire to burst into tears is a reaction of fear. Nor is the sense of guilt here a *feeling* of guilt. This is rather a far more metaphysical claim, the loss of innocence, not for a particular crime and not before a particular human tribunal, but that loss of innocence that comes from being judged, and recognizing oneself as being judged, by anyone or anything. It is Sartre's "look" *(le regard)*, through which we become brutally aware of others. It is this "look," bursting upon Meursault's life as a trauma, that is so terribly regarded by Clamence in *The Fall.* For him, the reality of other people's judgments, even the judgment of a sourceless laugh in the street or the possible judgment yet made by no one of an act unperformed (his failing to try to save the life of a drowning woman), is sufficient to collapse the delicate structure of unreflective innocence. His response is vindictive: "judge that ye not be judged." Meursault's guilt is Clamence's guilt, "Christian" guilt in the sense that mere awareness of oneself is in itself sufficient cause for damnation.

The function of the Kafkaesque trial, on this interpretation, is to force Meursault to reflect on his life, not to try him for murder. This is why the focus of the trial is not a plea of self-defense, which would have been reasonable and convincing (against an Arab with a knife who had already stabbed a friend, in a country already exploding with anticolonial resentment). . . . Accordingly, it is artistically and philosophically (even if not legally) appropriate that Meursault is tried for not weeping for his mother, for his friendship with a pimp, for his "liaison" with a woman. In each case, he is forced to see for the first time what his unthinking habits and relations appear to be "from the outside." (E.g. " . . . he kept referring to the 'the prisoner's mistress,' whereas for me she was just 'Marie.'") It is true that the trial is a political mockery, but its purpose is not to demonstrate some perverse injustice or to make a victim out of "innocent" Meursault. It is a trial of Meursault's uneventful life, not for justice, but in and for himself.

With reflection, Meursault begins to talk about his feelings, and his lack of feelings. Ironically, it is only at this point that he finally *has* feelings. At first simple feelings, boredom, vexation, hope, then annoyance and frustration, and finally, full-blown anger. He begins to understand desire. In Part I, all that he would want he has. It is only with deprivation that he learns what it is to desire. When Marie visits him in prison, he still says he has everything that he wants. This is not a lie on his part, but a symptom of his still primitive ability to reflect, and consequently to want. A bit later, he realizes that he cannot smoke in prison. (We were hardly aware that he did smoke in Part I.) At first he suffers faintness and nausea. Then he comes to understand that "this is part of my punishment . . . but by the time I understood, I'd lost the craving, so it had ceased to be a punishment."

It is with desire and frustration that Meursault begins to be a philosopher. At first he is "hardly conscious of being in prison," but he soon finds himself facing the awful breach between the concrete but vacuous reality of his former existence and the abstract but rich possibilities of thought. At first it is simple daydreaming, "my habit of thinking like a free man," but soon imagination begins to take the place of lived experience, and imagination, as we know from Descartes, Kant, and of course from Sartre, is the beginning of all philosophical reflection. At first, Meursault's philosophy is imitative and adolescent, at best: "One of mother's pet ideas . . . in the long run one gets used to anything." It is with his increasing frustration that his philosophy matures. In the half-humorous dialogue with his jailer, Meursault learns of *freedom,* now lost. It is with the sudden deprivation of his everyday routines . . . that reflection sets in. It is with the loss of the freedom which Meursault never knew he possessed that the "Why" of philosophy begins. It is only with the frustration of his desires that he begins to ask what is worth desiring. It is only with the lack of life's routine that life becomes a problem ("how to kill time"). To avoid frustration and boredom, Meursault invents a routine, a purely reflective routine. He practices remembering the contents of his room at home. And it is at this point that the most dramatic philosophical turn of the book occurs: "So I learned that even after a single day's experience of the outside world a man could easily live a hundred years in prison." Here is the final twist: reflection no longer serves experience, but experience serves reflection. One lives in order to be able to reflect, and now "life" is over. ("A life which was mine no longer.") Accordingly, Meursault's only conception of an afterlife is "a life in which I can remember this life on earth."

With the loss of freedom and the loss of "life" in this peculiar sense, Meursault can, like Sartre's damned trio in *No Exit,* view his life in its entirety. Like Clamence in his own "hell" in an Amsterdam bar, he can pass judgment upon it. The fact that he is also condemned to death by the court becomes almost incidental, a vehicle to insure that his reflections are not contaminated by *hope,* that his judgment is not moved by the possibility of "living" once again.

Meursault's gain of self-consciousness is at the same time a transcending of self. Once he begins to reflect on life, it is not simply *his* life itself. It is not his execution, but the idea of execution that puzzles him. It is not his death that torments him but death itself. In reflection, Meursault becomes, as Sartre once said of Camus, a "Cartesian of the absurd.". . .

WHY LIFE IS WORTH LIVING AFTER ALL

In the shadow of death, Meursault's reflections tend towards but inevitably fall short of the suicidal conclusion that Camus attacks in *The Myth of Sisyphus:* "It is common knowledge that life isn't worth living anyhow." For Meursault, the meaning of life resides only in the spontaneous and momentary lived experiences of Part I. In Part II, Meursault learns that his lost immediacies, the sun and sand, the smell of brine and Marie's hair, the taste of *café au lait,* were valuable in themselves. ("I'd been right. . . . ") To the chaplain, Meursault replies that "all his certainties were not worth even a single strand of a woman's hair." The value of reflection, in its turn, is just this understanding, reflected in Meursault's unique conception of an afterlife. In other words,

Meursault perversely sees that, on reflection, it can be seen that reflection is worthless. It is here that Meursault is more persuasive than his philosophical creator, for he has no pretentions of creating a second value—over and above "life"—in the very reflection within which life can be seen to be without value. Life is not of value *for* anything, yet it is worth living for itself. But Camus, not Meursault, adds another value, "keeping the absurd alive" [or as he writes in *The Myth of Sisyphus*] "a matter of living in the state of the absurd." Because Meursault is condemned to death, he will not be in a position to live in defiance and revolt. For Camus, the loss of prereflective innocence appears more terrible than a sentence of death. For Sisyphus and Clamence and, one might argue, for Camus himself, reflective defiance soon turns to scorn and resentment.

For Meursault, reflection is not cold and deliberate. It climaxes in "a great rush of anger, which washed me clean, emptied me of hope." Emotion and reflection, it seems, not emotion and innocence, go together. It is in the impassioned hopelessness of reflection, just before his execution, that Meursault faces "the absurd" as a final revelation: "Gazing up at the dark sky spangled with its signs and stars, for the first time, I laid my heart open to the benign indifference of the universe. To feel it so like myself, indeed, so brotherly, made me realize that I'd been happy, and that I was happy still."

How different is Meursault's "benign indifference of the universe" from Camus's "revolt of the flesh" [in *The Myth of Sisyphus*]. And how different is Meursault's acceptance of it from Sisyphus' scorn and struggle and Clamence's vicious bitterness. For Meursault, there is no "mind and world straining against each other," but a recognition of identity and "brotherliness." The universe itself, like Meursault, is unreflectively "indifferent." One might take note, however, that this proposition, as soon as it is stated by Meursault, becomes self-refuting. Meursault is perhaps the only character of Camus's creation, including the author himself, who knows the "happy death" that is his constant theme. "With death so near, Mother must have felt like someone on the brink of freedom, ready to start life all over again . . . And I too, felt ready to start life all over again."

Now what are we to make of this? Is it inconsistent with all that has gone before it? What could it mean in this context "to be free" or to "start life all over again"? Meursault's euphoric indifference is a falsification of his emotion, like Camus's calling Sisyphus' scorn of the gods his "happiness," like Jean-Jacques Rousseau, the philosophical champion of innocent "indifference," portraying his bitter resentment as righteousness and even joy. Something has gone very wrong, for the "feelings" to which Meursault is supposed to be faithful are not as they seem. If readers identified with Meursault in Part I (as I once did) for his honesty, this does not show that he does not lie but only that we too, like Rousseau, are pleased to fancy our innocence beneath a veil of social conventions and reflected sentiments. And that is a lie. And if readers are moved (as I once was) by Meursault's acceptance of an unjust death, this does not show that "he is willing to die . . . for the sake of the truth," but only that we too would like to be "innocent" even after committing a murder, satisfied with our lives even in the face of absurdity. But that too is a lie. Meursault, who was created with a paucity of feelings, dies with a feeling that is fraudulent. But given his hope to be hated ("all that remained to hope was that on the day of my execution there should be a huge crowd of spectators and that they should greet me with howls of execration"), he failed to be true even to that.

The Birth of Existentialism and the Death of Meursault

Patrick McCarthy

Patrick McCarthy, professor of European Studies at the Johns Hopkins University School of Advanced International Studies in Bologna, Italy, writes that the last chapter of *The Stranger* represents Camus's attempt to make his readers come to terms with their own inevitable mortality. Through the example of Meursault, who struggles against his imminent death, Camus comments on the ineffectuality of any human efforts at understanding death, including religion. McCarthy claims that this chapter in some way represents the end of the notion of God for Camus and also presupposes later developments in existentialist philosophy.

The final chapter has been described by one critic [Carl Viggiani] as 'an interpretation of what has preceded, a summing up of the knowledge gained'. The allusions to fatality which are scattered throughout the book take shape in what Meursault called 'the mechanism' that will terminate his existence. In Part 1 death was wrapped in lyricism and, while Meursault the character was saved because others died in his stead, Meursault the narrator defended himself with his ambiguity. There is no such ambiguity in the last chapter, nor is there much irony, for Meursault can no longer outwit his enemies by humour. Now he has to find a new language and in fact he discovers two: an attempted meditation on his own extinction and a cry of revolt.

There is fresh doubt about the sequence of this chapter because the first page is written in the present tense, which leads [Canadian critic Brian T.] Fitch to argue that it is chronologically the last moment of the book, that the interview with the priest has already taken place and that Meursault is now writing his journal. This may well be true, although one remembers that *The Stranger* takes some care to prevent us from understanding when and how it has been written. As for this chapter, it may be read, as Viggiani has suggested, as a separate entity where unity lies in the clash of extremes: the way that an extremely intellectual discourse breaks down and triggers an emotional outburst.

MEURSAULT'S ATTEMPTS AT ESCAPE FROM DEATH

The number three stands at the outset—'For the third time I refused to receive the chaplain'—to remind us that we are outside history and that the political struggle of Part 2, Chapters 1–4, is over. Meursault's awareness has grown and he is focusing it on his forthcoming end. He himself puts it differently: 'What interests me at this moment is to escape the mechanism'. But the trouble is that he cannot escape it and the structure of his meditation is that a cycle is repeated five times. Each time Meursault seeks to divert his mind from death but each time he is brought back to it.

The first time he thinks of escape and spins out a tale of books on escape—fabulous, unread and unwritten texts that depict last-minute flights—and then he concludes: 'But, all things considered, nothing allowed this luxury, everything denied it to me, the mechanism took hold of me again'. The difference between this language and the rest of the book is that doubt has now vanished. The usual formula of 'all things considered', which used to announce an awareness stranded in uncertainty, here announces the categorical statement emphasized by words 'nothing' and 'everything'. Meursault has attained certainty by coming up against his own limits.

Unable to confront this—'despite my good will I could not accept this insolent certainty'—he spins out a second flight which avoids the imminence of death by demonstrating that the penalty was imposed arbitrarily; but this tale has as its conclusion that, arbitrary or not, the decision is final. There follow similar tales where Meursault imagines that he is a spectator at the execution, that the guillotine might not work or that, since it is high above the ground, it is an imposing and noble edifice.

It is not fanciful to suggest that Camus is here explaining the ground rules of his own fiction, which refuses to accept the imaginative 'world' as the equivalent of reality. By using the language of analytical thought—the guillotine is described as 'a work of precision'—he undercuts the tale-telling of traditional novels. Meursault, who has always distrusted imagination, is thrown back on reason which offers him, however, an equally unsatisfactory discourse.

His next subterfuge is to plunge into his fear: 'the most reasonable thing was not to force myself'. Yet he retains control, even if the reader feels already that the breakdown is near. First Meursault imposes on his mind the target of surviving past dawn—prisoners to be executed are taken out at dawn and then during the day he juggles with his appeal, imagining now that it is accepted and now that it is rejected. The distinctive feature of these exercises is their intellectual rigour, which is forced on the reader's attention even as its tenuous control is equally stressed: 'Therefore (and the difficult thing was not losing sight of all the reasoning that this "therefore" represented)'.

Meursault's task, which is also depicted in *A Happy Death*, is to compel his sane mind to face death. Whereas most people combat death with the consolations of having played a role in a larger historical process or of perpetuating themselves biologically via their children, Meursault confronts it alone. Whereas most people are racked with pain, bewildered by age or befuddled with drugs, Meursault is healthy, young and in full possession of his faculties. His loneliness is accentuated by the way he specifically rejected Marie—'outside of our two bodies which were now separated nothing bound us together'. Indeed it is because this meditation refuses the usual non-transcendental forms of consolation that it forces the reader back to God and constitutes—in my opinion—religious writing.

Meursault's rigour is designed to compel man, a creature defined by his desire for immortality, to confront his mortality. This is what Camus will call 'the absurd' in *The Myth of Sisyphus*, where the confrontation will be handled differently. Here Meursault is tested by his conversation with the priest.

THE ROLE OF THE PRIEST IN *THE STRANGER*

Although he enters without permission and although he is yet another false father, the priest is not to be dismissed as a mere adjunct of the state. The conversation of Part 2, Chap-

ter 1, depicts the crucifix-wielding magistrate as a false
priest who deploys clichés. In a banal parody of pious jargon
he invites Meursault to become 'a child whose soul is empty
and ready to welcome anything'. But this time the priest is
not to be dismissed with easy irony.

He offers two kinds of arguments: the existence of sin and
the impossibility of a world without God. In secularizing the
concept of sin, by refusing to admit anything more than that
society considers him guilty, Meursault is rejecting the
framework of theological values that embraces sin. The
term has no meaning unless one also believes not merely in
free will but in grace and forgiveness, which in turn presupposes a loving God. This leads easily to the affirmation
(shared by Camus) that God does not exist and to a further
affirmation (unshared by Camus) that desire for immortality is 'no more important than wanting to be rich, to be able
to swim very fast or to have a better-shaped mouth'.

Against transcendental values, Meursault asserts the kind
of life he had lived in Part I and of which he became gradually aware in Part 2, Chapters 1–4. When the priest asks him
to perceive in the prison stones 'a divine face', Meursault
replies that he has only ever seen there Marie's face and that
he can now see only the stone. Stone, which is in Camus's
work associated both with happiness and distress, is here an
image of earthly life, and this is the life which Meursault asserts against the priest. Enraged at the illusion he is being
offered, he breaks into the cry: 'Something broke inside me
and I started crying at the top of my voice'. Like the Arab
woman, he begins with a denunciation, when he insults the
priest and insists that he does not want to be prayed for.

The language of this cry is a variation on ordinary
rhetoric. Questions, repetitions and antitheses abound although the clauses are short and the vocabulary is simple.
The weakness of these pages lends credence to [French
critic Jean] Gassin's contention that the book's ending is not
convincing, although one might argue that this discourse
should be read not for itself but as the metaphor of a cry
which cannot exist inside the pages of a book, and which is
echoed by the 'cries of hatred' with which society will greet
Meursault's execution.

After denouncing the priest, Meursault repudiates as in-
tellectualizations all judgements, whether moral or religious. The verb 'to understand' is used in a new sense. It is

the priest who is being challenged and who fails to understand—'Did he understand, did he understand this?'—while Meursault is in possession of wisdom. This consists in being able to articulate a preference for the flux of sensory experience and a refusal to categorize: 'I had lived in one way and I could have lived in another. I had this and I had not done that. I had not done one thing while I had done another. So what?'

The Stranger ends as Meursault affirms the worth of his daily round on the Algiers streets, a life that is both alienated because of the seeming absence of values and honest in its refusal of illusions. Non-intelligibility is changed by the act of recognizing and choosing it. In this way *The Stranger* offers the reader an early version of French Existentialism, which further explains the book's success.

But if this is the last word of such an elusive text, then it must be qualified in two ways. First, a wisdom that involves reflection on as well as involvement in concrete existence will surely strive to draw values from that reflection. *The Stranger* ends with an outburst where the simplicity of the language is a barrier against this development, but elsewhere such wisdom must spawn new moralities and ideologies. This will take place in Camus's other books, especially in *The Myth of Sisyphus.*

The second qualification is present in *The Stranger* itself and has to do with the vexing issue of oneness. In the last two pages the lyrical language returns and sensations of light, noise and smell take on a significance that is more than physical: 'Sounds of the countryside rose up to me. Odours of night, earth and salt refreshed my face. The marvellous peace of this sleeping summer came flooding over me'. This is different from the images of Part 1, Chapters 1 and 6, for no terror is involved and nature is not hostile, but is in sympathy with Meursault's revolt against the priest. Indeed it contains a language that is intelligible to him: 'in the face of this night full of signs and stars I opened myself for the first time to the tender indifference of the world'.

So the experience of oneness marks not merely that death is near but that some kind of truth or harmony has been attained. Meursault does not develop this theme and the lyrical vein is less strong than in the earlier passages. Moreover, he ends on a note of dualism, because he imagines himself going to the guillotine amidst the cries of hatred. However, the special insight into his condition which he expresses in these last pages is linked with the moment of oneness.

Hard as it is for me to define this experience with simple language and without injecting into it religious content, it is equally hard not to believe that Meursault's statement that the desire for God is no more important than desiring to swim well is misleading. It is the awareness of some sort of harmony that enables Meursault to appreciate both the happiness and the shortcomings of his absurd existence. This is surely why he compares himself with Christ on the final page: 'So that all may be consumated'.

Christ was God and man, and Camus believed he was chiefly the latter. But Christ is an uninteresting figure unless He retains some tiny trace of the Godhead, and this trace is what lurks behind the 'night full of signs'. At the very least the absence of God is not to be forgotten or overcome. And this in turn means that the final chapter of *The Stranger* does not merely sum up the rest of the book—and does not really fit with Part 1, Chapters 1 and 6—but looks outward to Camus's other books.

Meursault's Pagan Philosophy

Robert J. Champigny

Robert Champigny, professor of French and Italian at Indiana University, was one of the most influential commentators on existentialist literature, having written extensively on both Camus and his contemporary Jean-Paul Sartre. He discusses Meursault in two different states of innocence: the innocence of childhood and the innocence of what he calls "paganism." Champigny agrees with the numerous critics who see Meursault as living in a state of preadolescent consciousness. Additionally, he views Meursault's temperament as similar to that of a number of pre-Christian Greek philosophers, especially Epicurus. The followers of Epicurus advocated the enjoyment of only simple pleasures in search of a serene state of mind, referred to in Greek philosophy as *aponia* or *ataraxia*. Meursault's "paganism" separates him from the Christian society that judges him because he advocates living life according to natural laws (*physis*) rather than the laws that society has decreed (*antiphysis*, or *nomos*).

The reader of Meursault's narrative often has the impression of dealing with a candid and thoughtful child. Meursault has maintained the virtues of childhood, spontaneity in particular. He has not fallen into adulthood. He possesses the virtues of childhood and not its vices, for instance the vice of mimicry which makes a preadult out of a child. He has maintained the virtues of childhood, not the virtues of adolescence: Meursault is no romantic.

Meursault's horizon is childlike. Space for him is limited to what he encounters each day. Time is limited to the moment, to a day, to the next day, to a week at most. He does not

Excerpted from *A Pagan Hero: An Interpretation of Meursault in Camus's "The Stranger,"* by Robert J. Champigny, translated by Rowe Portis. Copyright © 1969 by University of Pennsylvania Press. Reprinted with permission.

turn his thoughts toward the past: it is only during his period of testing in prison that he attempts to make use of memories. He appears as an individual without a past, as a flat and transparent strip of glass.

When the prosecutor exploits the fact that Meursault has never "expressed any regrets," Meursault remarks: "I would have liked to try explaining to him cordially, almost affectionately, that I never really had been able to regret anything. I was always absorbed by what was going to happen that day or the day after it."

He easily abstracts himself from an unpleasant day in order to dream about more agreeable things awaiting him. Returning from his mother's funeral, he tells of his "joy when the bus entered the nest of lights of Algiers, and when I thought that I was going to go to bed and sleep for twelve hours."

His need of sleep and his aptitude for falling asleep when a waking moment offers him nothing of interest, this animal wisdom, may similarly be indicative of childish traits. We see him sleep in the bus which is taking him to the asylum where his mother has died, we see him sleep during the wake for his mother, and he falls asleep on the beach. In prison he manages to sleep "about seventeen or eighteen hours a day."

The desire to enjoy the moment goes with his horror of wasted time. The comedy of his trial, this adult comedy to which he is subjected, enters into his category of wasted time. He prefers sleeping to participating as his role of the indicted criminal demands: "All the useless things I was doing in this place rose to my throat again, and all I wanted was for it to be over so I could get back to my cell and sleep."

If a moment is wasted and if he cannot sleep, he has nothing left but boredom. It is not a question, as I have already noted, of romantic ennui, but of a childlike boredom, in terms of a particular moment: "He was boring me a little, but I had nothing to do and I was not sleepy."

Instead of collecting stamps he clips certain things from the newspapers: "Somewhat later, in order to have something to do, I took an old newspaper, and read it. I cut out an advertisement for Kruschen salts and pasted that into an old notebook where I put things from the papers that amuse me." This happens on a Sunday, a day which Meursault dislikes, as French children generally do.

I have already mentioned his acceptance, and in certain cases his understanding of, social conventions and proprieties. Here again he adopts a childlike attitude. A child adopts and sometimes understands the rules and conventions of adult society. But (at least if we are discussing a healthy child) he does not internalize these rules; he assumes no responsibility for them. Meursault's use of the expression "not my fault" is revealing. He is aware of the responsibility with which he is charged, but aware of it as something conventional and objective. He knows, rather than assumes, this responsibility. He knows that he is held to be a responsible person; but he does not feel responsible himself in cases which concern the observance of convention:

> I told her that Mother had died. As she wanted to know how long ago, I answered, 'It was yesterday.' She seemed embarrassed, but said nothing. I wanted to tell her that it was not my fault, but I caught myself because I remembered I had already said that to my boss. It could mean nothing. In any case, one is always somewhat at fault.

Like a child he experiences difficulty in managing conventional formulas. When characterizing the attitudes of other people toward him he uses two adjectives, of which the second especially strikes a childish note: "nice" and "mean." He finds a man with whom he is walking "very nice" to him. During his contentions with "justice" he appreciates moments when people "are not mean" to him. The attitude and the words of the prosecutor cause him to say, "I had a stupid need of crying because I felt how much those men detested me."

But people can also approach him as companions in a game, as individuals with whom it is possible to maintain natural, authentic relationships. Swimming in the sea with Marie, he experiences that concord only a well-played and wordless game may establish: "The water was cold and I was happy to be swimming. Marie and I swam away together from the beach and I felt that we greatly shared our moving together, and were content."

Yet Meursault is not a child, or rather, from the point of view I have chosen, he is not just a child. Maintaining the virtues of childhood while eliminating its vices implies reflection and a kind of training. The narrative contains one allusion concerning this point. This allusion permits the inference that Meursault was tempted during his adolescence, that he came close to falling into adulthood. His employer has just reproached him for having no ambition. Meursault then makes what is almost his only confidence about his past: "When I was a student I had a good deal of that kind of ambition. But when I had to give up studying, I very quickly realized that all that had no real importance."

Thus Meursault has shaped a certain conception of life, one differing from that of almost all other adults, who are content with the conception which was prompted into them. Meursault's conception will be explicitly and openly assumed on the last page of the narrative.

I have already spoken of Meursault's "pagan" temperament. It is appropriate to clarify what I mean by that term. Meursault's paganism will be presented as a development of what I have called the virtues of childhood. The Greeks have often been compared to children. What I have said so far about Meursault may recall the words of [German philosopher Friedrich] Nietzsche, according to whom the Greeks were superficial because they were deep. But these remarks are not adequate to clarify the meaning I propose to give to the word "pagan."

I indicated previously that by "pagan" I mean non-romantic and non-Christian. I have remarked that romantic dissatisfaction, the sense for and desire after the infinite, an infinite desire, a sentiment of the disproportion between the subjective and the objective, the sense that subjectivity is the fundamental mystery, that all this which is eminently romantic is not in the least applicable to Meursault.

Unbounded desire cannot generally be content with the offerings of perception. A romantic turns back to memory, toward poetic memory, to nostalgia: the [German] word *Sehnsucht* means both nostalgia and desire. Now, I have remarked that Meursault is not preoccupied with memories except during his hours of imprisonment, and that he is preoccupied then, not by nostalgia, but by particular memories, by memories which he might turn to practical use. Romanticism also makes a cult of the imagination: the word "imagination" is doubtlessly the best rallying-banner for romantics. Meursault admits, on the other hand, "I never had a real imagination." The images that he attempts to call forth in his cell are precise, and he has a practical purpose in mind. Meursault is a "realist." He is interested primarily in what is perceived, in whatever presents itself concretely to him at a given moment. If what presents itself is poor or disagreeable, "boring," he calls upon sleep. If he cannot sleep, then only and as a last expedient does he resort to memory or fancy. Poetic, creative exaltation, which is at the heart of romanticism, is foreign to him.

The distinction between "pagan" and "romantic" counts little for the rest of this study. On the other hand, I must at greater length make the distinction between "pagan" and "Christian" explicit. My intention is to present in terms of that perspective the opposition between Meursault and formal society, in particular the opposition between Meursault and the examining magistrate, then the chaplain.

In describing the conception that Meursault develops of life as "pagan," I refer to Greek thought. But so general a reference is inadequate because Greek thought is very diverse. It was by building upon certain Greek thinkers that Christianity grew into a theology. Moreover, if one abandons philosophy for mythology, one finds in Greek literature myths which do not lack resemblance to the Judeo-Christian myths of Creation, the Fall, of afterlife and judgment. Finally, the word "Christian," after so many centuries of evolution, ramification, and compromise, has become able to signify almost anything, and no matter what. To present an example of some import to this study, should I consider the words attributed to Jesus, "Who is my mother?" as marked with the Christian spirit; or am I instead to credit the authority of the cult of the family, particularly the person of the mother, which the Christian priests have encouraged? Another example: Jesus is said to have counseled his disciples to become as children. But I have suggested that by maintaining the virtues of childhood Meursault had implicitly taken up with a pagan conception of life.

DEFINING "PAGAN" AND "CHRISTIAN"

My intention in using the words "pagan" and "Christian" is not to define paganism as one category and Christianity as an opposite category, a task before which the historian of ideas would recoil. To justify my use of the two terms, suffice it that I shall present on one side a grouping of ideas which can be recognized as clearly pagan and not Christian, and on the other a second grouping which can be recognized as clearly Christian and not pagan. I do not presume to reach the essence of either paganism or Christianity, assuming that they can have an essence. In order to avoid misunderstanding, I shall speak in terms of "my pagan" and of "my Christian."

The notion basic to "my" pagan is that of *physis* [also known as "natural law" or "law of the jungle," the opposite of societal or "civilized" law]. He both affirms *physis* and questions it. Physis is all-embracing, opposed by nothing, at least on the fundamental plane. My pagan participates in the order of this physis, yet he can emerge from it, separate himself from it, and manifest it badly, thus placing himself in a state of "unrighteousness." My pagan's moral principle is the following: live according to physis.

My Christian minimizes the import of the notion of physis, or rather he retains no sense of it. Physis for him becomes nature, and that nature is interpreted as the creation of a being called God. My Christian partakes both of nature and of the divinity. He was created in the same way as other creatures, but God created him in His image. What once was physis for my pagan is divided into spirit and matter, or into soul and flesh. My Christian's existence in the midst of matter is the consequence of the "Fall" of his earliest ancestor. My Christian feels that he is an exile within material nature. This split between my Christian and nature is borne out by the myth of Incarnation and redemption. God made Himself into human flesh in order to save my Christian, though not the animals or the plants. The paradise to which my Christian aspires is an *antiphysis,* a Society, a Divine City.

My Christian's God is personal. He is not simply the divine. The domain of persons takes form apart from the rest of creation. A moral order is distinguished from the natural order. There are natural laws, and then there are ethical commandments.

In order to distinguish what is a person from what is not a person, my Christian speaks of the soul. My Christian's soul is quite different from the psyche of my pagan. My Christian has not arrived at a pure conception of subjectivity: he is not a Romantic. If the soul of my Christian is not an object for other persons, at least it is a "spiritual" object, an object of knowledge for his God. My Christian's soul is midway between my pagan's psyche and a romantic subjectivity.

My pagan defines himself as an animal endowed with logos: my Christian is defined as a fallen soul. From the beginning, my pagan feels innocent; from the beginning, my Christian feels guilty. My Christian is responsible for his soul in the eyes of his God. My pagan is responsible in his own eyes insofar as he possesses logos, that is, intellect and language. By the use of this logos, he may grow in tune with physis, or grow out of accord with it. So far as he is in accord, my pagan is a sage. My Christian attempts to resemble his God. If he succeeds, he is a saint.

My pagan is in pursuit of happiness, the means for which is a knowledge of physis. The love of wisdom is a love of knowing or of comprehending, and its end is happiness. A moral fault is not distinguishable from an intellectual fault. It is caused by error and ignorance. Unhappiness is the result of a discord; it is not always traceable to bad luck.

The morality of my Christian is not one of happiness. His morality is ambiguous. It can be interpreted as a morality of duty: my Christian's duty is to attempt to resemble his God, and his method is to obey the commandments attributed to his God. My Christian's morality may also be interpreted as an ethics of salvation: his goal is beatitude after death. The redemption of my Christian is not dependent upon his obeying the ethical commandments that he attributes to his God. His salvation depends upon faith in Jesus Christ, because through the power of Christ my Christian can be saved. It is not so much in terms of virtue as in terms of how a sinner believes and repents that my Christian may gain his salvation: the God of my Christian loves repentance. Thus what is efficacious is not knowledge or comprehension, but belief and repentance. However, my Christian can never be certain of his salvation, for it is supposed that God alone is able to judge his soul. The God who judges is a personal God, capable of intervention into the natural order which He created: providence, grace, ordeal.

Meursault is in clear opposition to two characters who profess Christianity, the examining magistrate and the chaplain. Among pagan doctrines, that of Epicurus is probably the one which Christians found most unfavorable. Meursault's temperament is Epicurean, though of course not in the vulgar meaning of the term. And his morality is Epicurean.

In composing "my pagan" I have relied upon Epicureanism. But, while it allows me to characterize Meursault's temperament and his wisdom, the Epicurean schema is not wholly adequate. For me, the atmosphere of the narrative occasionally evokes tragic and Ionian echoes.

Having laid the foundations of the "pagan" schema, I am

now in a position to describe Meursault's character, his temperament, his morality, and his conception of life in a coherent manner.

Negatively, Epicurean happiness consists of the absence of physical and mental suffering: aponia and ataraxia, [respectively]. Positively, happiness consists of pleasure, in "the judgment of nature itself, when nothing has already depraved it, and when it is expressed in all its purity and naïveté." It is a question of maintaining one's innocence and spontaneity.

Epicurus distinguishes between natural and necessary desires, natural but unnecessary desires, and unnatural and unnecessary desires. These last are practiced in the field of social antiphysis, of formal society: ambition, vanity. It is fitting to divest oneself of these parasitical desires in order to pursue the satisfaction of natural desires. In an ordinary situation, this is not difficult: "Nature is easily contented by limited goods, which are few in number and easy to acquire."

Meursault has divested himself of unnatural desires. This is shown in a passage already cited: "When I was a student, I had a good deal of that kind of ambition. But when I had to give up studying, I realized very quickly that all that had no real importance."

Expressions such as "I don't care" or "of no importance" occasionally encountered in the narrative might give the impression that Meursault is totally indifferent. In fact, one ought to speak of ataraxia rather than indifference, one ought to speak of an absence of perturbation. Meursault can seem indifferent only because he has become disentangled from unnatural desires, and it is these unnatural desires which ordinarily are described in written language. These desires, being social, are closely tied in with the emergence of the language of communication (though not of the language of pure and simple expression).

Meursault is not encumbered with ambition. Similarly, he seems devoid of vanity, though not of dignity: he has no social vanity, and his dignity is natural. He could not be troubled with that unnatural desire to marry which preoccupies Marie, nor could he, like Marie, consider marriage as a grave thing.

Meursault has razed useless superstructures within himself. Passion (excepting a fundamental passion which reveals itself to him after his condemnation to death) does not threaten to compromise his ataraxia, his openness to concrete reality. Marie asks him if he loves her. He answers negatively because he understands that by "love" Marie means something other than liking. Meursault is not in the least indifferent, even where people are concerned. For example, he tells his lawyer that he was fond of his mother and that he wishes that she had not died. But his mother's death did not overwhelm him: "I explained to him that my nature was such that my physical needs often got in the way of my feelings. The day we buried Mother I was worn out and very sleepy."

A better expression of this is that sentiments do not interfere with his physical demands, that passions do not trouble his ataraxia, that social desires are not substituted for his natural desires. What are Meursault's natural desires? Hunger, thirst, sleep. Natural still, though unnecessary (as he discovers in prison), is a desire to smoke, and the desire for physical love. Basically there is a desire not to suffer physically, the desire for aponia.

In the course of his narrative Meursault conscientiously notes his pleasures and his vexations: his liking for *café au lait* and the quality of the coffee offered him by the concierge at the rest home, the cigarettes he smokes, his stiffness and fatigue during the wake, an aching back here and an aching neck there, the pleasures of rest, of swimming, and of lunching on the beach. The following is reminiscent of Socrates deriving pleasure from scratching:

> Before leaving the office for lunch, I washed my hands. At noon I like this moment. Evenings, I enjoy it less because the rolling towel that the machine uses is quite damp from being used all day. One day I brought this to the boss's attention, and he answered that he was sorry but that it was, after all, a rather unimportant detail.

What is important to the employer is ambition, and not the quality of the towel. The social theatre is important to the employer, though concrete reality is not.

Meursault does not consider himself an actor among other actors on the social scene so much as a living individual among living individuals in the midst of nature. He places a neighbor and his dog on the same plane as living creatures: "They seem to belong to the same race, and yet they hate each other. . . . For eight years they have not changed the course of their daily walk. . . . They both stop on the sidewalk and watch each other, the dog with terror, the man with hate."

MEURSAULT'S NOTION OF PLEASURE IN EPICUREAN TERMS

Meursault is sensitive not merely to what is usefully pleasant, he is also sensitive to aesthetically pleasant things. He is sensitive not only to a particular phenomenon, he is sensitive to atmosphere, to the present totality out of which a particular thing emerges. His glance is inclusive as well as divisive. Meursault is penetrated by physis in its encompassing presence. At such times he is reminiscent of the Ionian vision. This sensitivity to a fundamental physis in its totality and in its power makes it possible for Meursault's life to be something other than a scattered collection of pleasures and boredoms, of isolated facts. This sensitivity will permit his life to take form within a tragic destiny, and will also permit Meursault to assume this unification of his life, that is, to become a hero.

During a court session, Meursault is withdrawn from the unreality about him by memories "of a life that belonged to me no longer, but in which I had found the simplest and most persistent of my joys: odors of summer, the neighborhood I liked, a certain evening sky, Marie's laugh and her dresses."

Let us single out the sky from this catalogue of pleasures. The reference is made over and again in Meursault's narrative. We are constantly aware that facts and things are placed in the framework not of the theatre, but of nature. Meursault spends the afternoon and evening of one Sunday contemplatively at his window, looking over human appearances in the street, appearances and disappearances coinciding with the passage of the day.

As in the Ionian view, the major presences in the narrative of this townsman are the sky and the sea, night and day, and above all sun and sunlight:

> I was blinded by a sudden splashing of light. . . . The brimming sunlight that made the countryside quiver rendered it inhuman and depressing. . . . I remained for a long time watching the sky. . . . I had the whole of the sky in my eyes and it was blue and gold. . . . The sky was green, and I felt happy. . . . It was good to feel the summer night flowing on our brown bodies. . . . Day, already full of sunlight, struck me like a slap. . . . The sunlight was falling almost from directly above on the sand, and its brilliance on the sea was unbearable. . . . The sunlight now was crushing. . . . I stayed at the first step, my head ringing from the sunlight, discouraged in advance by the effort it would require to climb the wooden

stairway and to approach the women. But because of the heat it was as painful to remain unmoving under the blinding rain of heat which fell from the sky. . . . I strained to overcome the sunlight and the opaque drunkenness that it poured over me. . . . An entire beach vibrant with sunlight crowded behind me. . . . A burning sword gnawed at my eyelashes and dug into my stinging eyes. Then everything lurched. The sea poured forth a thick and ardent breath. It seemed to me that the sky was opening over its entire expanse to let loose a sheet of flame. . . . The harsh light which poured into the windows from the sky and glanced around in the room. . . . Facing that night filled with signs and stars, I was opening myself up for the first time to the tender indifference of the world.

It can be seen that Meursault is not always capable of enduring the violence of physis, of maintaining his place within it. There will be error and tragedy. Meursault's tragedy, from the crime through its "analysis," its liberating assumption, is social only in appearance. Meursault must reject this appearance in order to assume the natural tragedy which is authentically his own.

Meursault adjusts to his imprisonment according to a wisdom which again might be called Epicurean:

I would wait for the daily walk that I made in the courtyard, or my lawyer's visit. The rest of my time was very well managed. I often thought then that if I had been forced to live in the dry trunk of a tree, with nothing to do except watch the bloom of the sky above my head, I would little by little have grown accustomed to it. I would have waited for the flocking of birds and the blending of clouds as now I would await those strange neckties my lawyer wore and as, in another world, I used to endure things until Saturday when I could clasp Marie's body. Now, to be fair about it, I was not passing time in a dried-up tree. There were people worse off than myself. That was one of Mother's ideas, and she had repeated it very often, that one gets used to anything in the end.

In his cell, he fights boredom by making an imaginary tour of the room in which he had lived:

I tried not to lose the thread of my inventory, to make a complete count. So that at the end of several weeks, I could spend hours just enumerating what was in my room. Thus, the more I reflected, the more forgotten and unappreciated things I could bring forth out of my memory. Then I understood that a man who has lived no longer than a single day could easily live a century in prison. He would build up enough memories to avoid boredom.

But Meursault encounters a fundamental difficulty when the death sentence has been passed against him. He still attempts to reason with himself, to continue the tactic which has succeeded up till now. He thinks of his petition for mercy:

> I always took the darkest possibility: my appeal had been turned down. 'All right, so I die.' Earlier than other people, that was evident. But everybody knows that life is not worth living. And I knew that whether you die at thirty or at sixty matters very little. . . . At that moment, what bothered me somewhat in my line of reasoning was the frightening leap I felt in myself at the thought of having twenty more years to live. But I could stifle that by thinking what my thoughts would be twenty years from now when I arrived at this same point. Since everyone dies, the how and the when do not matter, that is obvious. Thus (and the difficult thing was not losing sight of all the reasoning that this 'thus' represented), thus I had to accept the rejection of my appeal.
>
> At that moment, at that moment only, I had, so to speak, the right, I gave myself permission to approach a second hypothesis: I was pardoned. The vexing thing about that was that I had to make the bound of my body and my blood—that spring which made my eyes smart with a mad joy—less ardent. I had to apply myself to lessening this cry, to reasoning. I had to be natural even in this second hypothesis, in order to make my resignation about the first more plausible. When I had succeeded, I would have gained an hour of calm. *This* was not to be ignored.

Meursault's wisdom here combats a difficulty of a special order. He has divested himself of particular passions. No passion for a defined object has gravely menaced his ataraxia. But now Meursault discovers in himself a passion for the total object, for the total object which is also a subject, which is himself as a living being: the passion to live. If, in the concluding pages of the novel, he manages to overcome this major obstacle, it is not in the manner that his Epicurean wisdom has triumphed over other ordeals. Epicurus emphasized the problem of the fear of death, but he may not have treated it in a fitting perspective.

Meursault will not strip himself of this passion to live, for it is the basis of his integrity. To adopt a purely Epicurean wisdom here would probably be to deny himself. Meursault maintains the exaltation of living: he will try to make himself equal to it. It seems to me that at such a time Meursault transcends the limits of wisdom: he becomes a hero. We are not yet in a position to approach that final Meursault.

CHAPTER 2

Technical and Historical Aspects of *The Stranger*

READINGS ON
THE STRANGER

The Theme of Death

Kathryn B. McGuire

Kathryn McGuire, instructor at the University of
North Texas, focuses on images of life and death in
the opening section of the book, in which Meursault
attends his mother's funeral. She notes that Camus
uses alternating images of light and dark to suggest
the intermingling between life and death that occurs
at funerals. McGuire also points out that a number of
the images Camus chooses for this section are reminiscent of mythological symbols relating to death
and old age. She also extends her analysis of the
symbols in this section to discuss their meanings in
psychoanalytical terms and how these interpretations reinforce Camus's themes.

The funeral vigil in Camus's *The Stranger* subtly illustrates
a primary, though paradoxical, existential tenet—that the
knowledge of death is the beginning of full awareness of life.
Through a series of antitheses that merge the images of
death/birth, sterility/fertility, and old age/infancy, Camus
denotes the physical conjunction of the antithetical sites
birth and death in order to point out that living, in an existential sense, lies neither in birth nor death, but is made possible out of their conjunction.

The antithetical imagery becomes apparent from the moment that Meursault enters the mortuary where Mme.
Meursault's body lies at rest, as Camus draws on a vast sym-
bolical field—the concept of light. Rather than being dark
and associated with the color black as befits a funeral, the
setting was "a very bright, whitewashed room, with a sky-
light for a roof."

As psycholinguistic studies reveal, light is equated with
consciousness, truth, insight, and enlightenment. Light also
suggests the human qualities of man, while darkness suggests nonbeing and the anxiety of death. The color white

Reprinted from "Camus's *The Stranger*," by Kathryn B. McGuire, *The Explicator*, vol.
50, no. 1, pp. 50–53, Fall 1991. Reprinted with permission from the Helen Dwight Reid
Educational Foundation. Published by Heldref Publications, 1319 18th St., NW, Wash-
ington DC, 20036-1802.

(the walls, the nurse's smock, the bandage on her face), although seemingly out of place in a funeral setting, can signify innocence, but at the same time, the paleness of death.

ECHOES FROM MYTHOLOGY AT THE FUNERAL VIGIL

Meursault is conducted through the funeral vigil by two ambiguous figures—a caretaker (Fr. *concierge,* Eng. *doorkeeper*) and a nurse (Fr. *infirmière*). According to Joseph Campbell's extensive studies of the heroic journey toward self-knowledge in mythology, the uninitiated individual had to pass through the bounds established by the threshold guardians into a new zone of experience. The mythological guardians acted as both instructors and barriers to the uninitiated. When the caretaker says that he is supposed to unscrew the coffin lid so Meursault can see his mother, giving him the opportunity to grasp the reality of her death, Meursault refuses.

As evening approaches,

> The caretaker turned the switch and I was blinded by the sudden flash of light. . . . I asked him if he could turn off one of the lights. The glare on the white walls was making me drowsy. He said he couldn't. That was how they'd been wired: it was all or nothing.

The caretaker suggests in the phrase "all or nothing" that we either live in light or dark; that is, we either grasp the reality of death or we don't, we either live in the moment of the perceptive now or we don't—there is no middle ground.

The nurse, one who normally takes care of the living, is "near the casket" as though guarding it. The caretaker explains her bizarre appearance:

> "She's got an abscess." I didn't understand, so I looked over at the nurse and saw that she had a bandage wrapped around her head just below the eyes. Where her nose should have been, the bandage was flat. All you could see of her face was the whiteness of the bandage.

Certainly, the bandage could suggest the mask worn by a surgical or delivery-room attendant, but the bandage also covers her mouth, implying that she cannot or will not communicate verbally. She sits with her back to Meursault, a position that imparts a certain secrecy, or at least inscrutability. In dream analysis, speechless silence is a familiar representation of death, for the dead cannot speak.

The nurse's mannerisms extend the ambiguity: "The way her arms were moving made me think she was knitting," an activity traditionally associated more with birth than death. But knitting is also suggestive of the stern and gloomy mythological goddesses Clotho, Atropos, and Lachesis [known collectively as "the Fates" in Greek mythology or "the Morae" in Roman mythology], who ruled the lives of men. According to Greek and Roman mythology, they spun and cut the thread of life.

The old people who come in to take up the vigil with Meursault "floated into the blinding light without a sound. They sat down without a single chair creaking." In mythological terms, once having crossed the threshold, the adventurer moves in a dream landscape of strangely fluid and ambiguous forms. The

CAMPBELL'S NOTION OF CROSSING THE THRESHOLD

Noted scholar Joseph Campbell studied myths from hundreds of different cultures and formed a general theory about the form of mythological stories by noting similarities among them. One of the similarities was that mythic heroes generally had to cross a threshold of some sort during their initiation into a changed, presumably for the better, state of being or knowledge. The excerpt below briefly outlines some of the characteristics of this crossing, which McGuire claims occurs in The Stranger *as well.*

With the personifications of his destiny to guide and aid him, the hero goes forward in his adventure until he comes to the "threshold guardian" at the entrance of the zone of magnified power. Such custodians bound the world in the four directions—also up and down—standing for the limits of the hero's present sphere, or life horizon. Beyond them is darkness, the unknown, and danger; just as beyond the parental watch is danger to the infant and beyond the protection of his society danger to the member of the tribe. The usual person is more than content, he is even proud, to remain within the indicated bounds, and popular belief gives him every reason to fear so much as the first step into the unexplored. Thus the sailors of the bold vessels of Columbus, breaking the horizon of the medieval mind—sailing, as they thought, into the boundless ocean of immortal being that surrounds the cosmos, like an endless mythological serpent biting its tail—had to be cozened and urged on like children, because of their fear of the fabled leviathans, mermaids, dragon kings, and other monsters of the deep.

Joseph Campbell, *The Hero with a Thousand Faces,* New York: World Publishing Co., 1956, pp. 77–78.

group of old people coming in silently at night also suggests mythological initiation rites in which the older generation's function was to give spiritual instruction and benign support.

The ten old people, plus the caretaker and the nurse, make up a body of twelve, suggesting a jury, and indeed they do seem to sit together in judgment of Meursault. The coffin separates him from the twelve. The dead mother in the coffin represents death/old age/sterility in the antithesis; Meursault represents life/youth/fertility; and the twelve onlookers represent the mediation point in the antithesis. Certainly, they are described in specifically antithetical terms. Meursault's surrealistic description of them begins with sexual allusions that suggest fertility:

> Almost all the women were wearing aprons, and the strings, which were tied tight around their waists, made their bulging stomachs stick out even more. I'd never noticed what huge stomachs old women can have. Almost all the men were skinny and carried canes.

The bulging waists of the old women suggest pregnancy, but the women are old and therefore sterile. The old men are carrying canes, which function as phallic symbols in psychoanalytical terms, but they too are old, withered, and sterile.

> What struck me most about their faces was that I couldn't see their eyes, just a faint glimmer in a nest of wrinkles. When they'd sat down, they looked at me and nodded awkwardly, their lips sucked in by their toothless mouths. . . . Now it was all these people not making a sound that was getting on my nerves. Except that every now and then I'd hear a strange noise and I couldn't figure out what it was. Finally I realized that some of the old people were sucking at the insides of their cheeks and making these weird smacking noises.

The wrinkles, of course, are consistent with a newborn's appearance as well as with an old person's. The "toothless gums" and the sucking noises reinforce the old age/infancy antithesis.

The old ones seem to "sit in judgment" of Meursault, who seems to sit in judgment of his dead mother, herself a site of antithesis, for the mother gives life, which is the beginning of death, and as death giver deserves Meursault's censure.

The end of the vigil implies that the mediation/initiation is complete: "On their way out, and much to my surprise, they all shook my hand—as if that night during which we hadn't exchanged as much as a single word had somehow brought us closer together."

The Algerian Context of *The Stranger*

Alec G. Hargreaves

Alec G. Hargreaves, senior lecturer in French at Loughborough University in England, discusses *The Stranger* in light of the wide range of responses it has provoked because of its uniquely Algerian characteristics. Hargreaves begins by sampling some of the more hostile reactions, especially those that accuse Camus of sympathy with the European (specifically, French) colonial domination of Algeria. While not necessarily clearing him of these charges, Hargreaves argues that Camus was more interested in philosophical matters than issues of race or nationality. However, he also points out that the historical realities of Algeria under French colonial rule do not allow for such an easy separation of themes.

In the last interview that he gave before his death, Camus was asked what aspects of his works had been unduly neglected by French literary critics. He replied: . . . "The obscure part, what I feel blindly and instinctively. French criticism is always first interested in ideas. But, relatively speaking, could you study Faulkner without reference to the South in his work?" Through this reference to the role of the American South in the writings of William Faulkner, Camus was clearly alluding to the importance of his native Algeria within his own works. While Camus mainly had in mind his emotional attachment to the topographic features of Algeria, other parallels with the American South also suggest themselves. Colonial Algeria, like the southern part of the United States, was characterised not simply by its geographical position in relation to an associated northern territory (which in Camus's case lay in France) but also by an ethnically diverse population and a history of political inequality. As Ca-

Excerpted from "History and Ethnicity in the Reception of *L'Etranger*," by Alec G. Hargreaves in *Camus's 'L'Etranger:' Fifty Years On*, edited by Adele King. Copyright © 1992 by Adele King. Reprinted with permission from St. Martin's Press.

mus rightly observed, the particularities of Algeria had initially attracted very little attention in critical studies of his works. *The Stranger* was seen primarily as an exploration of man's universal condition, summed up in the notion of the absurd. Within a year of Camus's death, the French historian Pierre Nora was to publish a radical reassessment of the author's first novel: . . . "His novel about the absurd does not dramatise a philosophical discovery, but the foundation of a racialist colony; it is the sublimated, purified expression of a real historical situation." A few years later Ahmed Taleb Ibrahimi, Minister of Education in post-independence Algeria, made a still more severe analysis of the novel: . . . "In killing the Arab Camus achieves, subconsciously, the dream of the *pied-noir* who loves Algeria but can only conceive of an Algeria without Algerians." By 1970, Conor Cruise O'Brien had produced the first general study of Camus to take as its pivot the author's colonial roots. Twenty years on, the re-evaluation of Camus's Algerian origins has continued to feature prominently in the numerous studies devoted to his work, especially *The Stranger.*

How are we to explain the diversity of these interpretations, and how are we to evaluate the significance of the Algerian factor within the fabric of *The Stranger?* If the first of these questions is slightly less difficult to answer than the second, the complexities of both are hinted at by a common thread running through the comments of Nora and of Taleb Ibrahimi, as well as those of Camus himself. All three specifically mention the importance of unconscious elements in the author's depiction of Algeria. The [literary critic] Hans Robert Jauss has emphasised the role of unconscious factors in shaping the 'horizons of expectations' within which texts are written and read. In producing or interpreting the text, writer and reader create patterns of meaning which depend on the assumption of certain types of knowledge, belief and desire. Changes in those assumptions, which are culturally and historically conditioned, may sharpen the reader's awareness of aspects of the text which were previously too self-evident to elicit comment or too deeply buried to be made manifest. In our analysis of *The Stranger* and of the divergent interpretations to which it has been subjected, we shall see that variations of this kind are intimately linked with a tide of historical change at the heart of which has lain the process of decolonisation. This tide has stimulated new readings in France and other Western countries. It has also brought the rise of new groups of readers in what we now call the Third World. From their different positions in time and space, Camus's readers have inevitably approached *The Stranger* with markedly contrasting horizons of expectations.

The review of *The Stranger* published by Sartre early in 1943 typified the line of approach which was to dominate scholarly studies in France for many years to come. Sartre, like Camus, shared with many European intellectuals a preoccupation with feelings of cosmic meaninglessness. In his review, Sartre makes only one reference to the ethnic particularities of Algeria, when he compares Meursault's seemingly arbitrary thoughts in Part 1 of the novel to a monotonous, nasal, Arab chant . . . one of those tunes of which Courteline remarked that "they disappear, never to return" and stop all of a sudden. The idea of Arab chants being meandering and meaningless is a reflection of Sartre's almost total ignorance of Algeria and its inhabitants. It was not until the Algerian war of independence, which began in 1954, that the inhabitants of metropolitan France began to have anything more than a fitful awareness of the conditions obtaining on the other side of the Mediterranean. Almost three million Frenchmen fought in that war, which for much of its duration ranked as the single most important preoccupation of the French public. Journalists and others turned expectantly to Camus, whose origins seemed to give him an unrivalled basis from which to comment on the conflict. His reluctance to do so puzzled many, and persuaded some that behind Camus's Algerian connections lay some guilty secrets. This shift of horizons among the French reading public prepared the ground for reassessments of *The Stranger* such as that undertaken by Nora.

The violence through which the French had established and attempted to sustain their presence in Algeria before granting independence in 1962 remains to this day a sensitive area in the self-image of France presented in schoolbooks and official government pronouncements. The continued emphasis given in French textbooks to the philosophical aspects of *The Stranger* has therefore been viewed with considerable suspicion in Algeria. Far from being an embarrassment, the struggle against French domination is for Algerians fundamental to their sense of nationhood. Government ministers such as Taleb Ibrahimi have helped to create a horizon of expectations in which Algerian scholars have found it natural to interrogate the political credentials of writers who, like Camus, had their origins in the *pied-noir* (settler) community. Within the English-speaking world, the most ambitious attempt at reinterpreting the whole of Camus's *oeuvre* in the light of his French Algerian roots has come from the pen of an Irishman. Situated on the very edge of Western Europe, Ireland may perhaps seem an unlikely position from which to initiate such an analysis. Bearing in mind the troubled colonial history which has characterised Ireland's relations with Great Britain, O'Brien's interest in parallel aspects of the Franco-Algerian relationship makes much more obvious sense.

While their historically situated nature helps us to understand the diversity of the readings to which *The Stranger* has been subjected, how are to we to gauge their relative merits? Is there not a danger of readers simply projecting back onto the novel personal preoccupations devoid of any intrinsic connection with the text? In assessing the worth of these various interpretations, explanatory comments made by the author may sometimes help, but it would be naive to regard external authorial pronouncements as automatically reliable or exhaustive. The test of any interpretative approach must ultimately be its purchase on the overall economy of the text itself.

Camus's Intent and the Algerian Reaction

In his review, Sartre shrewdly underlined the paradoxical contrast between the apparent lack of structure in Meursault's thoughts and the highly structured form of the text, in which each seemingly insignificant event in Part 1 is eventually used in the legal case brought against the narrator-protagonist in Part 2. Meursault's view of the world and the death sentence which is passed upon him serve, in Sartre's reading, to make of *The Stranger* an orderly work, composed about the absurd and against the absurd. Is this quite what the author was aiming at? I don't know. I am simply presenting the reader's opinion. It is clear from Camus's notebooks that the formal structure remarked upon by Sartre had indeed been deliberately designed by the author to articulate the theme of the absurd: . . .

> It is a carefully planned book, with a deliberately chosen tone. I wanted my character to reach the only great problem

through what occurs daily and naturally. The meaning of the book resides precisely in the parallelism of the two parts. Conclusion: society needs people who cry at their mother's funeral; or else you are never condemned for the crime you think you will be.

The absurd—the apparent meaninglessness of life in the face of human mortality and the absence of any transcendent God—is implicit in Meursault's reactions to events in Part 1. The nature of this, the only great problem, is cruelly confirmed by the seemingly rational but in fact arbitrary interpretation placed upon his behaviour by the prosecutor in Part 2, and is articulated explicitly in Meursault's confrontation with the prison chaplain in the final chapter of the novel. Meursault has by then become convinced that his is a universal condition shared by all human beings, and this view is clearly endorsed by both Camus and Sartre. In reality, *The Stranger is* far more culture-specific than the author on Sartre suggests. As Camus notes, the novel leads the protagonist and the reader to its allegedly universal truths "through what occurs daily and naturally", i.e. through the depiction of spontaneous and seemingly ordinary social experiences. The everyday world portrayed in *The Stranger* is that of colonial Algeria. Camus's aim was to use self-evident aspects of that world as a peg on which to hang his universal theme. Yet things are never truly self-evident: they only appear so to certain observers. What Camus takes for granted serves in practice to mark the ethnic and historical position from which he speaks.

The very notion of the absurd as a universally-felt human condition is itself indicative of the ethnic divide which stood between Camus and most of Algeria's inhabitants. Had they been able to read Camus's novel, it is highly unlikely that the Muslims who accounted for the overwhelming majority of the Algerian population would have recognised themselves in its picture of cosmic meaninglessness. The godless universe inhabited by Camus was that of a twentieth-century European; it was light years away from the Islamic beliefs adhered to by most Algerians. Few of the Muslims living in Algeria in Camus's day were capable of reading *The Stranger,* for after more than a century of colonial rule education remained the preserve of the minority settler population, together with a small native elite. Most Muslims therefore remained as ignorant of European thought as did

Camus, or for that matter Sartre, where the ideas and beliefs of non-Europeans were concerned. Sartre's description of Arab chants as meandering and incomprehensible is an obvious mark of this ignorance; such chants would appear wholly natural and coherent in Arab ears. Sartre was of course a native of metropolitan France and had never set foot in Algeria, so his lack of instruction in North African culture is perhaps hardly surprising. Granted that Camus had been born and lived practically all his life in Algeria, his ignorance of the Arabic language and of Islamic culture in general is far more striking.

Camus always claimed to feel a deep affinity with Algerians of non-European descent, and was proud to have campaigned for improvements in their lot during his early career as a journalist. The road to the improvements which Camus wished to secure for the Muslims lay through assimilation. This long-established colonial doctrine meant in theory that the indigenous inhabitants of France's overseas empire would be turned into fully-fledged Frenchmen, with the same culture, living standards and political rights as the settler population. In practice, the seemingly generous notion of assimilation was bedevilled by a number of intractable problems. Firstly, the lofty rhetoric of the civilising mission was matched on the ground by very few economic resources (hence the low levels of educational provision in colonies such as Algeria). Moreover, settlers anxious to retain their privileges were positively opposed to any moves which would give equal political status to non-Europeans. Finally, even apparently sincere assimilationists such as Camus implicitly took the view that indigenous cultures were of lesser value than French civilisation; the arrogance inherent in that view rather took the edge off the generosity of spirit often associated with assimilation. Although Camus never acknowledged his commitment to full-blown cultural assimilation, his deepest instincts undoubtedly lay in that direction. It is true that while explicitly supporting political and economic assimilation, Camus would sometimes add that the cultural traditions of non-Europeans merited serious respect. More commonly, however, he urged during the 1930s that all of Algeria's inhabitants should come together in a new Mediterranean culture. Whenever he defined that culture, it consisted almost exclusively of European ingredients. Islam was conjured away in a silent disappearing trick;

in Camus's eyes it clearly did not appear as natural as the European presence in Algeria. Later, during the war of independence, he would depict Islam as a force fundamentally irrelevant to the true interests of the Algerian people. Wedded as he was to the idea of French sovereignty in Algeria, Camus simply could not bring himself to accept that Muslims might legitimately define and pursue an entirely independent identity of their own.

Algeria had been brought under French rule during the nineteenth century by military conquest. A people subjugated by force of arms and vastly superior to them in numbers was hardly a reassuring presence from the point of view of the *pieds-noirs*. The beauty of assimilation (in theory, at any rate) was that it appeared to make the 'native problem' vanish: by turning Algerians into Frenchmen, the threat to the French presence in Algeria was removed. In an article published alongside that of Pierre Nora, and which directly anticipates Taleb Ibrahimi's analysis, Henri Kréa (a writer of mixed French-Algerian descent) was to see in *The Stranger* a much more violent version of this disappearing trick: . . .

> When Meursault, 'the stranger', fires on 'the Arab', he magically kills a racial entity in which he is afraid of being dissolved. This action, which he believes is caused 'by the sun', is the subconscious realisation of the obscure, childish dream of the little white man that Camus never stopped being.

During his trial, Meursault denies that he intended to shoot the Arab, and blames the killing on the sun. While Kréa may doubt the sincerity of these assertions, there is every reason to suppose that Camus intends the reader to believe them. In his preface to the American edition of *The Stranger*, as in the extract from his *Carnets* quoted earlier, Camus suggests that Meursault is convicted not for having murdered an Arab but for having failed to cry at his mother's funeral. The same point is made by Meursault in his conversation with the priest. The prosecution case against Meursault in Part 2 rests on a monstrous but seemingly rational interpretation of the events depicted in Part 1. The author undoubtedly intends the reader to see in Meursault an innocent man unjustly condemned to death. Within the economy of the novel, this conclusion flows inescapably from both the ideology of the absurd and the narrative structure so carefully thought out by Camus.

THE ARGUMENT AGAINST A COLONIAL READING

It is therefore difficult to substantiate the notion that *The Stranger* embodies an unconscious genocidal urge, for there appears to be no role for such an impulse within the main fabric of the novel. The story does, however, make significant use of the inter-ethnic tensions which characterised colonial Algeria. Meursault finds himself with a gun in his hand facing a hostile Arab as a consequence of his friendship with Raymond. Raymond's brutal mistreatment of his Arab mistress, which provokes the confrontation on the beach, is surely emblematic of the historical rape inflicted on Algerian Muslims by the settler population in general. While Meursault does not share Raymond's enthusiasm for initiating violence, he has no qualms where self-defence is concerned. In the first of two skirmishes which precede the shooting, it is one of the Arabs who makes the first aggressive move and who draws first blood by using his knife on Raymond. In the second incident, Meursault tells Raymond that he cannot use his gun unless the knife is first drawn once more. When, in the final confrontation, Meursault faces one of the Arabs alone, he does not shoot until after the knife has been drawn. The obvious inference to draw from all this is that the shots fired by Meursault are a justified response to the threat posed by the Arab.

It is tempting to see in this arrangement of the story evidence of an underlying consent, on the part of the author, to the defence of the French presence in Algeria by force of arms. For many, this commitment appeared to become explicit when, at the height of the war of independence, Camus declared that he would if necessary defend his mother rather than justice in Algeria. Yet while readers of *The Stranger* may see in the text evidence of legitimate self-defence, neither Meursault nor his lawyer makes such a case explicitly. Within the overarching framework of the absurd it is important that the killing of the Arab should in fact defy rational explanation; hence Meursault's baffling references to the sun. It is in this sense an arbitrary killing. Implicit evidence of self-defence helps subtly to strengthen the image of innocence attaching to the protagonist, but the primary source of that innocence is shown to reside in the metaphysical absurdity which permeates his existence.

The injustice visited upon Meursault by the court is an image of that which is inflicted on all human beings by virtue of their mortal condition: the death sentence which is imposed on each and every one of us seems as arbitrary and unjust as that to which Meursault falls victim. Yet to sympathise with Meursault the reader must condone or at the very least disregard his equally arbitrary killing of another human being. There seems to be a double standard at work here: the injustice inherent in the shooting of the Arab is implicitly deemed to matter less than that involved in the execution of his killer. It is true that, unlike the prosecutor, Meursault does not intend to kill. Somewhat more disturbingly, however, he seems equally detached from the killing after the event. At no point does he express regret over the death of the Arab. Camus clearly intends his readers to share Meursault's indifference towards the murdered man; otherwise they will find it impossible fully to sympathise with the protagonist when the court orders his execution. In what ways do the killer and his victim differ? Apart from his movements on the beach, we are told practically nothing about the dead man. His only distinguishing feature is that he is an Arab, whereas Meursault is a European. Perhaps it is this that accounts for his lesser worth.

Like Meursault in *The Stranger,* Patrice Mersault, the protagonist in Camus's early novel, *A Happy Death,* feels innocent despite the fact that he has killed a man. The victim in *A Happy Death* is a cripple who conveniently describes himself as half a man, thereby reducing the significance of his death. The murdered Arab in *The Stranger* hardly seems to qualify as a man at all. The Arabs in Camus's novels are always nameless, shadowy characters, and as a number of commentators have observed, this tends somewhat to depersonalise or even dehumanise them altogether. We have already seen from external sources that although Camus never admitted it, at an unconscious level he took a dismissive view of Algeria's Islamic culture. The assumption that non-Europeans were inferior was so widespread when *The Stranger* was written that for most white men it literally went without saying. Opinions differ as to whether, in writing the novel, Camus was aiming primarily at a *pied-noir* audience or at readers in metropolitan France. Bearing in mind the virtual non-existence of a Muslim public sufficiently educated to read his works, Camus must certainly have assumed that his readership would consist essentially of Europeans, whether on the northern or the southern side of the Mediterranean. In the colonial period, it seemed self-evident that the death of an Arab was less important than that of a European. Camus may not have consciously thought in those terms when constructing the plot, but the exoneration of Meursault in the eyes of many readers was undoubtedly made very much easier by the ethnicity of his victim.

Among the most recent monographs devoted to *The Stranger* is that of Patrick McCarthy. The horizon of expectations within which he approaches the novel is markedly different from that of Camus's earliest readers. From his post-colonial vantage point, McCarthy singles out Camus's treatment of the Arab for special attention. He finds it 'hard to imagine that the author . . . could have chosen to write a novel where an Arab is murdered, without brooding on his choice of victim.' Yet there is no evidence in Camus's published notebooks or correspondence to show that he made such a carefully considered decision. His main concerns were of a quite different, philosophical order. In fictionalising them he seems to have drawn on social attitudes and assumptions which hardly needed thinking about at all. Within the overall fabric of the novel, the shooting of the Arab is no more than an instrument through which to set up Meursault's trial on a charge sufficiently serious to carry the death penalty. Through this sequence of events, Meursault and the reader are eventually brought face to face with what, in his *Carnets,* Camus described as "the only great problem," namely the absurd. But by casting an Arab as Meursault's victim, the author approached his "universal" theme via attitudes and experiences of a much more localised nature. Camus appears to have assumed that in the eyes of most readers, the inherent inferiority of Arabs and the threat which they were felt to pose to Europeans would reduce or even eliminate any element of guilt attaching to Meursault. As an Algerian scholar has recently observed, there is a deep irony in the fact that in emphasising Meursault's innocence, Camus cannot universalise the central problem articulated in *The Stranger* without . . . committing an injustice against the colonised Arab.

CHAPTER 3

The Stranger in Comparison with Other Works

Race in *The Stranger* and Richard Wright's *Native Son*

Mary Ann Witt

Produced in roughly the same time period, *The Stranger* and Richard Wright's *Native Son* both center on a protagonist who is simultaneously an insider and an outsider to his own country. Mary Ann Witt, professor of foreign languages and literatures at North Carolina State University, compares Bigger Thomas's social standing as an African-American in white-dominated Chicago with that of Meursault, an Algerian of European descent in a predominantly Arab country. She isolates a number of ways in which their stories overlap, but also focuses on the important distinction between them that results from the differing degree of social control possessed by the minority groups to which they belong. Witt argues that both characters refuse the status assigned to them and thus cause their own downfall.

Meursault and Bigger Thomas, both created on the eve of the Second World War and later labeled as existentialist antiheroes, have remarkably similar careers. They are "native sons" of the countries where they live, Algeria and the United States, but, as members of a racial minority, strangers in those lands. They are also social and metaphysical outsiders, alienated from the religious and cultural values of their own racial and social group. Both lead limited lives. Each is fatherless and has a paradoxically close and distant relationship with his mother. Each is sexually involved with a girl, but indifferent toward love or marriage. Fortuitous circumstances lead Bigger and Meursault to kill a member of the racial majority of their respective countries.

Excerpted from "Race and Racism in *The Stranger* and *Native Son*," by Mary Ann Witt, *The Comparatist: The Journal of the Southern Comparative Literature Association*, vol. 1, no. 1, 1977. Reprinted with permission.

Each is imprisoned, tried and sentenced to death by a court representative of the power structure of his society which condemns him more because of what he is than because of his alleged crime. The condemned man in both cases violently rejects the appeal of a Christian minister and ends by facing death alone with a heightened sense of awareness and a new sureness of himself.

The similarity of situation and destiny in the protagonists of *Native Son* and *The Stranger* is a structural one lying well beneath widely divergent character portrayals, styles, plots, themes and purposes. Richard Wright's novel belongs to the American proletarian genre of the thirties and has a (slightly heretical) Marxist axe to grind; Albert Camus's belongs in the tradition of, if in revolt against, the French psychological novel and contains no dogma other than the author's developing sense of the "absurd." The portrayals of white racism and of the black man's situation in mid-century America were central to Wright's purpose, and race is accordingly a dominant theme of *Native Son.* The racial theme is secondary and much more subtle in *The Stranger.* It went unnoticed until several years after the novel's publication and has still not received much critical attention. A comparison between the treatment of race in these structurally similar novels should shed some light on each.

The gulf between Arabs and Europeans in colonial Algiers appears as wide, if of a different order, as the gulf between black and white Americans in mid-century Chicago. Both Camus and Wright portray societies in which members of one race do not really communicate with members of another race, indeed do not view them as human beings. Although *Native Son* is more grounded in the tradition of realism than *The Stranger,* the portrayal of race and racism in both cases deviates considerably from realism. Both the deterministic way in which the protagonist's destiny is treated and the use of symbols from nature characterize the styles of the two novels, in very different ways, as extensions of naturalism. Wright and Camus are less interested in providing documentary examples of racial antagonism than in portraying its existence on a symbolic level. Because of this portrayal they have both been charged with racism—a charge unjustifiable unless one somehow identifies exposure of a situation with adherence to it.

Let us state an obvious difference between the two pro-

tagonists at once. Although Meursault and Bigger Thomas
are both members of racial minorities, the former belongs,
in [French-African philosopher] Franz Fanon's terms, to the
race of the colonizers and the latter to the race of the colonized. Both men are apolitical, even asocial, but they instinctively reject the situations assigned to them. Bigger will
not accept the "place" allotted blacks as his mother does;
Meursault astonishes the colonial power structure by refusing to play its game or conform to its values. Yet each is also
conditioned by his racial and social group. Since the novels
are written primarily from the protagonists' point of view,
the reader perceives Arabs as Meursault perceives them and
whites as Bigger perceives them. In both cases the other race
appears as largely inhuman. Wright and Camus emphasize
its nonhumanity by the use of images from the natural,
inanimate world. The racial theme in both novels is handled
in essentially two ways: 1) through a symbolic framework
identifying members of the racial majority with nature and
2) through the tragic destiny of the protagonist as it is affected by that framework. We shall examine these methods
in that order.

THE PORTRAYAL OF "THE OTHER"

Many readers of *Native Son* have observed that its white
characters are surprisingly one-dimensional. Mr. Dalton is
the entrepreneur-philanthropist; Mrs. Dalton the well-
meaning but morally as well as physically blind white lib-
eral; Mary the theoretical but class-bound leftist; Buckley,
most caricatural of all, the "politician" and blatant racist.
Only Mary's communist boyfriend Jan and, to a lesser extent, Bigger's party-chosen lawyer Max emerge with some
sort of individuality and even they are defined primarily,
like characters in a melodrama, by their roles. In contrast
Bigger, his mother, Bessie, and even lesser characters like
the boys in Bigger's gang are portrayed in their full human-
ity. This has been seen as a defect in the novel. If there is a
defect here, however, it lies in Wright's failure to maintain
Bigger's point of view consistently throughout. The stereo-
typed nature of the white characters makes aesthetic sense
only in those terms. In answering early critics of *Native Son*
who had proclaimed that he "hated whites," Wright re-
minded his readers that from Bigger's viewpoint, whites
were indeed *not* real human beings. The fact that Bigger and

his kind are viewed as subhuman by whites is stark and obvious; it permeates every action of the novel. Wright's intention to portray the corresponding (or resultant) non-humanity of whites from Bigger's point of view is carried out not only through stereotyping, but also through the more successful technique of repeated images which finally give the reader a symbolic vision of Bigger as a lone human tragically pitted against powerful, inanimate natural forces.

Wright prepares the reader, with a rather too obvious authorial interjection in Book I, for the symbolism equating white people (from Bigger's point of view) with forces of nature which he will develop throughout the novel. "To Bigger and his kind white people were not really people; they were a sort of great natural force, like a stormy sky looming overhead, or like a deep swirling river stretching suddenly at one's feet in the dark." Bigger's lawyer Max, during the trial in Book III, recapitulates the point when he explains that American blacks facing whites "feel that they are facing mountains, floods, seas: forces of nature whose size and strength focus the minds and emotions to a degree of tension unusual in the quiet routine of urban life." This symbolism is developed to its greatest intensity in Book II, in which Bigger is pursued by what seems to be most of the white population of Chicago during a driving snow blizzard. [American critic] Keneth Kinnamon has counted 101 references to snow in the novel, all but three in Book II. The reader's consciousness of the relentless snow leads him to expect the ensnarement of the lone black man by the hostile and powerful white world. This is of course what happens: at the end of Book II, Bigger is pushed into the snow by his white captors as he is identified with Christ—a symbol which will be developed in Book III. "Two men stretched his arms out, as though about to crucify him; they placed a foot on each of his wrists, making them sink deep down in the snow."

Other motifs carry the symbolism identifying white people with forces of nature. The figure of Mrs. Dalton hardly appears as a human being at all but as a "white blur"—a sort of threatening, ghost-like fog—and the Dalton's white cat, also a "white blur" with accusing green eyes, watches Bigger stuff Mary's body into the fiery furnace. Jan and Mary first appear to Bigger as "two vast looming white walls," and the white race in general becomes "that white looming mountain of hate."

The symbolic presence of the looming mountain or the driving snow makes itself felt throughout the novel. The barrier which separates the races is broken through only by an act of violence. It is only after Bigger has killed the woman Jan loves that the latter begins to perceive him as a man more than as a representative of the black proletariat and Bigger in turn sees in Jan something beyond the white race. But even Bigger's experience of accepting a white man as a fellow human for the first time in his life is described in this way: "a particle of white rock had detached itself from that looming mountain of white hate and had rolled down the slope." The tragic sense which permeates the novel stems from the unequal nature of the opponents. What can one individual do against a great natural force? Bigger strikes out against it in vain fury; the white liberals and communists make attempts to alleviate it. The efforts are humanly touching but, in a larger context, inadequate: will any number of rolling stones break down a mountain? And is not Jan still more a "white rock" than a comrade? We are not even given the assurance that a revolution would make any difference—in this sense Wright's communist critics were justified in their perception that *Native Son* does not adhere to party line. The symbolic framework of the novel remains a tragic one.

If the white people in *Native Son* are one-dimensional, Arabs in *The Stranger* are given no character portrayal at all. Their most striking feature is their silence. Camus uses Arabs as a kind of backdrop belonging to the natural world against which the human drama of Europeans is played. The European drama becomes linked to the Arab world through Raymond's relationship with a "Moorish" girl, which leads to Meursault's unwitting involvement in a small racial war.

The first Arab to appear in the novel is the nurse with a tumor whom Meursault observes knitting in the morgue during the wake for his mother. The race is next mentioned when Meursault remarks that Raymond's mistress must be "*une mauresque*" ["a moorish woman"]. On the morning of the killing, after Meursault has helped Raymond with his "revenge," he sees the Arabs he will later meet on the beach across the street from his house. When Meursault steps out of his building, the sun hits him "like a slap in the face." When he sees the Arabs, he describes them in this way: "They were staring at us silently, in the special way these people have—as if we were blocks of stone or dead trees."

Since these two metaphors are the only ones in the passage, the gaze of the Arabs becomes associated with the sunlight striking Meursault. It seems, in Yeats's words, "as blank and pitiless as the sun." The metaphoric description of the Arabs' stare serves a double purpose: it shows that Meursault is aware that the Arabs do not perceive their colonizers as human beings, and it shows that Meursault sees the Arabs more as part of the inanimate than of the human world. As Meursault, Raymond and Marie leave to catch their bus, Meursault again perceives the Arabs as a silent, immobile part of the natural scene: "They were exactly as before, gazing in the same vague way at the spot where we had been."

The association between Arabs and the natural world, in particular the sun, in the climactic scene of the novel will be analyzed in detail in the discussion of the racial implications of Meursault's destiny. Suffice it to say here that the Arabs on the beach remain a silent part of the natural world of heat, sand and water, pitted against the human, conversing Europeans. Meursault's last view of the man he kills is of a "dancing image" in the "flaming air." And his reaction after he has pulled the trigger is not "I killed a man," but "I knew I'd shattered the balance of the day."

Ironically, Arabs are first (and only momentarily) perceived as human by Meursault after he has killed one, as Bigger and Jan were only able to communicate after the death of Mary. When Meursault is first sent to prison, he is put in a big room with "mostly Arabs," and the following brief, rather strange scene takes place.

> They grinned when they saw me enter, and asked me what I'd done. I told them I'd killed an Arab, and they kept mum for a while. But presently night began to fall, and one of them explained to me how to lay out my sleeping mat.

It has been suggested that the Arabs grin because they are rather surprised and delighted to see a European taken prisoner, and thus brought to their level. But why the gesture of solidarity, even after they know that Meursault has killed one of them? Do they see Meursault, beyond his race, as just another prisoner? Or has the act of killing itself somehow tentatively broken through the wall between the races?

Arabs are soon to return to their non-human role in the novel. The scene in the visitors' room, where Marie comes to see Meursault, is particularly significant in its portrayal of the two races. The Europeans in the scene are referred to as "men," "women," "prisoners," or "visitors"; the others are called "Moorish women" (mauresques) or "Arabs." For example, Marie is "surrounded by Moorish women" but the "small old woman" and the "fat matron" next to her, observed with some detail, turn out to be Europeans. We are told that because of the distance between the grills, the "visitors" and the "prisoners" had to speak very loudly, but then we learn that the "Arab prisoners" and their families were squatting opposite each other, talking in whispers. "This murmur of voices coming from below made a sort of accompaniment to the conversations going on above their heads." The visiting room of the prison is like a miniature portrait of Algerian society as it appears throughout *The Stranger*. The "murmur" of the Arabs makes up a quiet, unintelligible, but constant bass to the "conversations" of the Europeans. The murmur is brought up again in a sentence just before one describing sunlight "surging up" against the window, giving the impression that both are part of a natural background on which the drama of "people" is played.

No more Arabs appear in the novel, and the victim of Meursault's crime is conspicuous only by the unusual lack of reference to him during the trial. He is referred to as "the Arab," twice by the prosecutor and once by Meursault, and as "the victim" by the judge. One would not expect the state's attorney in a colonial court to stir up emotions on behalf of a native victim, but one might expect his opponent to enter a plea of provocation and self-defense. If such an argument would better fulfill the demands of realism, it would not be in keeping with the portrayal of the Arab in the rest of the novel. Since he is not perceived as human, the Arab cannot be ascribed a motive for attacking Meursault. The native Algerians remain a silent backdrop, part of an enduring natural world on which a temporary, uneasy and defensive social structure has been placed.

In the symbolic framework of *Native Son*, the majority race is viewed by the "colonized" as an aggressive force of nature, a looming mountain or a driving snow, and in *The Stranger* the majority race is perceived by the colonizers as a passive but threatening African heat. Both protagonists come up against these natural forces and are destroyed through them. Meursault's situation is more complicated and more isolated because he shares in the European view of Arabs as nonhuman, and kills partly because of it, but in a way he allies himself with the natural world of the colonized in rejecting the artificial social one created by the colonizers. Bigger can at least identify himself with the black and oppressed, but his revolt against his own kind comes in the form of a rejection of the safe, resigned and religiously oriented world of his mother and of the majority of blacks. The revolt of both men against their situations as colonized or colonizer is, until their imprisonment, instinctive rather than conscious and is conveyed to the reader through images and the impulsive responses of the protagonists to them.

THE ROLE OF A MINORITY IN A HOSTILE SOCIETY

The images to which Bigger responds in Book I of *Native Son* are those generated by a capitalist economy and a racist society—images of forbidden and therefore highly desirable objects. Idling on a street corner with his friend Gus, Bigger watches an airplane circling in the sky and remarks that he could be an aviator if he had "a chance." It is not really a chance to enter aviation school that interests Bigger (or his creator) but a symbolic perception of the black man's lack of freedom. Bigger transfers this perception to another image:

> Goddammit, look! We live here and they live there. We black and they white. They got things and we ain't. They do things and we can't. It's just like living in jail. Half the time I feel like I'm on the outside of the world peeping in through a knot-hole in the fence.

The image is appropriate to Bigger's entire existence and seems to prefigure his destiny. The novel opens in the cramped, one-room apartment of the Thomas family and closes in a jail cell, thus framing the reader's perception of Bigger by an association with the trap in which he has always been caught. Imprisonment on death row is in a sense Bigger's logical end and the jail merely a physical embodiment of a long-standing situation.

Bigger's response to another image generated by American society sets him on the path which will ultimately lead him to be trapped by it. Shortly after observing the airplane with Gus, Bigger attends a typical thirties movie displaying the luxurious living of upper-class whites. Bigger reacts to his impulsive wish to enter this never-never land by rushing to apply for a job as chauffeur with the Dalton family which his mother and sister had urged him to take for quite different reasons. Bigger's actions in the Dalton household are characteristic of his relations with the white world: they are prompted by a combination of desire, hatred and fear. These impulses become crystallized in his reactions to the idealistic leftist family daughter, Mary Dalton. Bigger cannot possibly see Mary as an individual woman, nor can he understand her political ideas. She is rich and white: therefore she is charged with symbolism. He hates and fears her because of what she represents rather than because of what she is. If he desires her, it is in the same way that he desires the chance to fly a plane or the riches and luxury in the movie. He desires her because she is forbidden, because as a white woman she is the object most forbidden by the white world to the black man. His desire for her, like his hatred for her, are both instinctive rejections of the "place" assigned to him. In that sense, as he will reflect later on, rape is indeed the appropriate symbolic name, although not the real one, for his crime against Mary, against the white world.

Impulsive reactions to images from the white world continue to characterize Bigger's life in Book I. These are crystallized in the climactic scene where Bigger's killing of Mary is accomplished through his response to the physical and symbolic presence of "the white blur," Mrs. Dalton. Standing by Mary's bedside, Bigger becomes terror-stricken when her mother appears in the doorway. Wright portrays him as literally possessed by the ghostly presence. "A white blur was standing by the door, silent, ghostlike. It filled his eyes and gripped his body." It is in this state of possession—"His eyes were filled with the white blur moving toward him" that Bigger unwittingly suffocates Mary. The "white blur" is mentioned twice again as the tension in the scene reaches its climax. Bigger regains consciousness, or frees himself from possession, gradually. Immediate realization of what he has done can only be seen in retrospect: "As he took his hands from the pillow he heard a long slow sigh go up from the bed into the air of the darkened room, a sigh which afterwards, when he remembered it, seemed final, irrevocable." It is only after Mrs. Dalton has left the room that Bigger examines Mary and discovers she is dead. He then sees himself as the symbol which the white world will make of him.

> The reality of the room fell from him; the vast city of white people that sprawled outside took its place. She was dead and he had killed her. He was a murderer, a Negro murderer, a black murderer.

The replacement of the verb of action "had killed" by "was" in reference to Bigger parallels the symbolic imposition of "the vast city of white people" on "the reality of the room." Bigger is aware of the moral judgment which will be made not only on his act but on his entire being—the adjective "black" has overtones beyond the color of his skin. The linguistic change in these sentences contains in synoptic form the major development of the rest of the novel. The act which Bigger performs in a state of possession will be transformed by white society into a revelation of his "being" for which he will be executed.

Book II of *Native Son* is characterized by Bigger's continued impulsive, fearful and hostile reaction to the white world, now an overwhelming symbolic presence in the snow, and by a new development of his reflective powers in his ability to plan his life, and to understand what he has done and what is being done to him. When Bigger is condemned in Book III, it will be more for rape than for murder. This is foreshadowed during Bigger's "flight" when, prompted by a question from his girl Bessie, he reflects on the symbolic nature of his crime against Mary.

> Had he raped her? Yes, he had raped her. Every time he felt as he had felt that night, he raped. But rape was not what one did to women. Rape was what one felt when one's back was against a wall and one had to strike out, whether one wanted to or not, to keep the pack from killing one. He committed rape every time he looked into a white face. He was a long, taut piece of rubber which a thousand white hands had stretched to the snapping point, and when he snapped it was rape. But it was rape when he cried out in hate deep in his heart as he felt the strain of living day by day. That, too, was rape.

From their own point of view, "the people of the state of Illinois" are right when they sentence Bigger Thomas to death for a crime which he did not commit. During the court proceedings in Book III the actual crimes committed by Bigger—the manslaughter of Mary, the rape and the premeditated murder of Bessie—are gradually disregarded while the prosecution focuses on Bigger's alleged rape of Mary. The climactic point of the plea made by Buckley, the state's attorney, comes when he declares: "He killed her because he *raped* her! Mind you, Your Honor, the central crime here is *rape!* Every action points toward that!" What the representatives of white society have done is to focus on a crime which symbolizes the essence of Bigger Thomas and it is for this essence that they condemn him. Buckley argues that Bigger is "sub-human," "beast-like," foreign to "our way of life" and to the laws of civilization.

The court condemns Bigger for a mode of existence which it rightly sees as a threat to its own model of "civilization." A place, like that of his mother's within the black ghetto, was cut out for Bigger Thomas. His instinctive desire for life beyond that place and his revolt against the limits imposed on him by white society merit, in its eyes, his expulsion.

WHAT HAPPENS TO SOMEONE WHO DOESN'T BELONG?

Meursault does not fit into a designated social "place" any more than does Bigger Thomas. But if Bigger is seen as a threat because he wants too much, part of Meursault's "strangeness" stems from the fact that he wants too little. Like Bigger, Meursault is before his imprisonment characterized by impulsive responses, but he is viewed as odd because he does *not* respond to images of success and luxury. As a lower middle-class white man in a colonial situation, Meursault is expected to aspire toward professional advancement, money, marriage, and to defend vigorously the institutions and values of the mother country. Yet this stranger responds more to a clean washroom towel than to his employer's offer of a promotion in Paris. He is more affected by the sun than by the ceremonies at his mother's burial and is able to put aside memories of the latter for a refreshing swim and a pretty girl on the following day. The Church and the Law, the two prime institutional representatives of the mother country in the colony, interest him not at all until he is forced by their effect on him to perceive their absurdity. Meursault's mode of living each present moment for itself, brought out by the style in the first half of *The Stranger*, may also be seen as a threat to the colonial mentality. A good colonist could not allow himself to live totally in the present: he needs constantly to reaffirm his link with the past and his expectations for the future. But Meursault's life is more intimately bound to the sun and the sea of North Africa than to European social institutions.

The native Algerians, as we have seen, are viewed in the symbolic framework of the novel as a part of the natural world on which a social structure has been imposed. Yet if Meursault instinctively rejects the colonial social world, he most certainly does not belong to the Arab one. If he is not a racist, he does seem influenced by what Renée Quinn has called a "collective attitude." He does not question the values of Raymond in his sadistic treatment of his "Moorish" mistress, but instinctively sides with him. His only speaking acquaintances seem to be European. And if Arabs are seen as largely inhuman throughout the novel, it is from Meursault's point of view.

Meursault's tragic destiny comes about at least in part because he is caught between two antagonistic racial groups and belongs to neither of them. His troubles begin when he transgresses the racial boundaries in becoming involved with Raymond's affair, and he is of course arrested for killing an Arab. Ironically, however, he is condemned for symbolic reasons that have far more to do with his failure to be a good colonist than for his manslaughter of a native victim.

As everyone knows, Meursault kills an Arab "because of the sun." The importance of the sun throughout *The Stranger* is obvious, and critics have assigned a wide variety of symbolic significance to it. One value of the sun, however, has not been sufficiently analyzed: the growing and intense association between Arabs and sunlight and heat during the fatal beach scene.

The confrontation between Europeans and Arabs on the Algerian beach may be viewed as a kind of ritual which repeats in increasing rhythmical intensity a motif which goes: sun, Arabs, violence. The scene is of course depicted from Meursault's point of view, and in his eyes the Arabs become gradually almost indistinguishable from the light and heat of the sun. Meursault's first view of the Arabs coming down the beach is preceded by his first observation of the "almost vertical" sunlight, the glare, and the heat on his forehead. Raymond, Masson and Meursault prepare themselves for a possible fight. Meursault then feels the intense "red" heat of the sand, and Masson and Raymond fight with the Arabs. As the Arabs back away, watching them, the three Europeans remain "nailed under the sun," associating the Arabs' gaze with the sun's heat. When Meursault follows Raymond onto the beach, he perceives the sunlight "splintering into flakes of fire" and then the two Arabs by the rock and the stream. At this point a brief relaxation of the mounting intensity, like an oasis in the desert, occurs. Meursault observes the two Arabs in some detail, one playing on a flute, and the other staring silently at Raymond. They blend perfectly into the description of the natural decor—the notes of the flute resemble the trinkling of the stream and the silent stare the relentless sunlight. The music and the flowing water offer such a contrast to the stark sand and heat that it almost seems as if some sort of truce will be reached. But Raymond puts his hand on his revolver, and as Meursault persuades him not to fire, the Arabs slip away.

When Meursault goes out alone, the sun's heat intensifies as the metaphors used to describe it multiply, Meursault is literally driven by the sun toward his victim as he vaguely thinks of escaping from its heat near the cool stream. The Arabs have become associated with nature both as refuge and peace and as violence and hostility. It is of course the latter that Meursault finds. His vision of the Arab becomes fused with his perception of the sun's heat: "one could see his dungarees steaming in the heat;" "I saw him as a blurred dark form wobbling in the heat haze." When the Arab pulls out his knife, he is totally obscured by the sunlight reflected on the metal. The climax, where the sun metaphorically attacks Meursault and the gun's trigger "gives," resulting in the Arab's death, has been prepared for by the repeated association of sun, Arabs and violence. Meursault is possessed by the sun's "cymbals" which beat on his forehead and its "sword" which stabs him in the eyes in much the same way that Bigger Thomas is possessed by a "white blur." Both men kill involuntarily, in a state of frenzy, striking out against a great natural force rather than against another human being.

Meursault's trial has very little to do with all this. The French colonial court is no more interested in prosecuting Meursault for killing an Arab than the Chicago court is interested in trying Bigger for the murder of Bessie. The "French people" like "the people of the state of Illinois" focus on a symbol which somehow defines the essence of the man they have chosen as a scapegoat. The symbol chosen by the American court is Bigger's "rape" of a white woman; the symbol chosen by the French court is Meursault's neglect of his mother and apparent indifference at her funeral. Why is this colonial arm of justice so interested in the defendant's relationship with his mother?

Meursault's mother, judging by occasional references in the text was probably as "strange" as he, and the court obviously has no interest in her particular person. It is rather the state of motherhood which seems to represent to the colonial establishment something vital to its own existence, something which Meursault's way of life seems to threaten. It is not only Meursault's disregard of social institutions, but also his refusal of continuity and causality, his "absurd" way of living each present moment for itself, which rubs against the grain of the representatives of State and Church. Motherhood, of all social roles, represents continuity and causality, or the link between present and past. The Mother is the fundamental unit of society; to colonists she may well represent *la mère patrie* [the mother country]. If Meursault can be more affected by the heat of the sun than by the sight of his mother's corpse, is he not capable of abandoning himself to the African present and forgetting the French past? Would he cry at the funeral of the mother country? The "crime" of which Meursault is accused—the "moral murder of his mother"—becomes to the court a symbol of Meursault's mode of existence just as rape becomes symbolic of Bigger's. The French colonists, like the white Americans, choose a scapegoat to expel.

The protagonists of *Native Son* and *The Stranger* may thus be seen, at least in part, as victims of racism and colonialism. As individuals, they succeed in transcending the traps in which their societies catch them through a new awareness of themselves and their destinies, a kind of inward freedom acquired paradoxically in prison. But this transcendence is a tragic one and the situations which caused the tragedies remain unaltered. Both novels expose a society composed of a race of "colonizers" and a race of "colonized" in which the members of each race do not view members of the other race as human beings. Meursault is in the highly ironical situation of being caught between the two antagonistic races. As a white European, he views Arabs as part of the inanimate natural world—he perceives himself as shooting at the sun and "shattering the balance of the day" rather than as killing a man. Yet he is condemned to death by the French colonists because he does not share their values or fit their expectations. He belongs with neither the oppressed nor the oppressors but remains alone. Bigger, on the other hand, clearly belongs to the oppressed race. He views members of the oppressor race as inanimate parts of a great natural force, and when he kills he perceives himself striking out against a powerful "white blur" rather than suffocating a girl who had tried to befriend him. He is condemned by the white court not simply because he is black, but because he refused to accept passively his role as one of the oppressed. He revolts against the members of his race who do accept that role and in that sense, like Meursault, he remains alone. Although race and racism are secondary themes in *The Stranger* and primary ones in *Native Son*, both Camus and Wright use a symbolic framework and the destiny of an anti-hero to portray a fundamental, tragic antagonism.

The Stranger and Kafka's The Trial

Willard Bohn

Considerable evidence exists that Camus had read Franz Kafka's groundbreaking novel *The Trial* (published posthumously in 1925) before he began working on *The Stranger*. Despite the numerous thematic and even structural similarities, Willard Bohn, professor of foreign languages at Illinois State University, cautions against simply reading *The Stranger* as a reworking of Kafka's book. The books share the common trait of forcing the reader into self-contemplation by demonstrating through their respective protagonists the undesirable results of not doing so. *The Stranger* is ultimately more optimistic about the possibility of finding some degree of existential understanding, but both Josef K. and Meursault serve as metaphorical sacrifices to help their creators impart certain lessons.

There are two reasons why a comparative study of Josef K., the hero of Kafka's *Der Prozess*,[1] and Meursault, the hero of Camus' *L'Étranger*,[2] is especially justified. First of all, from external evidence it seems highly likely that *L'Étranger* was influenced by *Der Prozess*. [American critic] Phillip Rhein summarizes the evidence as follows:

> At precisely the time Camus was reworking his novel, he was keenly interested in Kafka. According to a letter from Camus, he read Kafka's *Der Prozess* in 1938. This is also the year that he reassembled his notes and began to work on the composition of *L'Étranger*. That he was greatly struck by Kafka's work is not only established by his letter, but Kafka's impression on him has been given definite form in the essay "L'Espoir et l'absurde dans l'oeuvre de Franz Kafka,"[3] as well as in his succinct appraisal of *Der Prozess* in the novel *La Peste*.[4]

1. *The Trial* 2. *The Stranger* 3. "Hope and Absurdity in the Works of Franz Kafka" 4. *The Plague*

Reprinted from "The Trials and Tribulations of Josef K. and Meursault," *Orbis Litterarum*, vol. 40, no. 2, 1985.

Secondly, because of the marked similarities between the two novels, a study of one automatically throws light on the other. At times *L'Étranger* seems almost a carbon copy of Kafka's book. Both works involve their heroes in absurd trials, both sentence them to death, both confront them with prison chaplains, both cause them to experience epiphanies shortly before death—the list of similarities continues indefinitely. . . . Choosing to analyse the forces governing the human condition, both works are necessarily structured around their protagonists, whose existential dilemma is that of mankind in general. Continuing the tradition of the *Bildungsroman*[5]—an inherently existential genre—both books stress the development of mind and character in their heroes. If Josef K. and Meursault have much in common, it must be admitted that they also differ in several important respects. They are not completely interchangeable. We will not go far wrong, however, if we take the following statement as our guideline: "Both artists see man as a stranger bound to an indifferent world: totally responsible for and singly witness to his own existence."

As the stories develop it becomes increasingly apparent that, like many existential heroes, our protagonists belong to what Northrop Frye calls the "ironic mode":

> If inferior in power or intelligence to ourselves, so that we have the sense of looking down on a scene of bondage, frustration, or absurdity, the hero belongs to the *ironic* mode. This is still true when the reader feels that he is or might be in the same situation, as the situation is being judged by the norms of a greater freedom.

K. and Meursault seem to be inferior to ourselves largely because they are completely and uncomprehendingly at the mercy of their predicaments—one is tempted to say environments. Josef K. is powerless to cope with or to understand the Law. Meursault is incapable of dealing with organized society (the trial) or with the effects of the sun. Moreover, he appears not to understand much of what goes on around him. What makes the situation particularly ironic is that the men who are caught in society's tangled web have spent their lives steering clear of any possible impediment to their freedom, of any real involvement or commitment. Both heroes are alone, detached from most of the normal human entanglements, drifting through life without permanent attachments or goals. Not only

5. a "coming of age" novel

are they still unmarried at the age of thirty or thereabouts, they are conspicuously lacking in relatives. K. was raised by his uncle, whom he sees infrequently—Meursault by his widowed mother, whom he likewise sees infrequently and who dies early in the novel. Similarly, neither character has any real friends. K. seems to have none at all, and while Meursault has Emmanuel, Céleste, and Raymond, they seem to be little more than casual acquaintances. Finally, neither has any real love interest. The relationships with Else and Leni are merely sexual conveniences for K., and though Meursault agrees to marry Marie he attaches no importance to it since he does not love her. Not only do both heroes spurn friendship and love, they do not really seem *capable* of such demanding relationships. K. and Meursault are essentially, passionless, self-centered, and unimaginative individuals. Moreover, they live exclusively in and for the present and the immediate future. They are interested only in the concrete and the physical, remaining oblivious to the spiritual and intellectual side of life. To be sure K. is intelligent, but when he exerts himself mentally it is with the sole object of obtaining concrete, practical results. Meursault, too, seems intelligent, but it is only toward the very last that he actually begins to exercise his intellect. In short, if we had to choose one word to characterize their state, that word would be *estranged.* K. and Meursault have little meaningful contact with the world about them, though superficially they appear to function satisfactorily because they are able to satisfy the mechanical requirements of their office jobs. Toward the end, K. cannot even handle his office work satisfactorily.

But of course there are many differences between the heroes too. Two very important characteristics of Josef K.'s, which Meursault does not share, are his obsession with reason and order and his delight in playing the petty tyrant. These qualities can best be viewed as the extension of his professional life into the domain of his private life. As Herbert Tauber remarks, "Die Stellung in der Bank gibt für K.s Verhältnis zum Dasein den bedeutsamsten Ausdruck. Die Laufbahn, das geschäftsmässige Verfolgen eindeutiger Zwecke, bestimmt nicht nur sein Berufsleben, sondern sein ganzes Wesen."[6] In other words, K. attempts to live his life as

6. "The job at the bank gives the most meaningful expression to K.'s relationship to existence. The career, the businesslike pursuit of meaningful aims, defines not only his work-life, but his whole being."

if the world were his office. The following quotations, necessarily limited, demonstrate his preoccupation with reason and order:

> . . . er musste jetzt nur diese Fähigkeiten, die ihm [his high position in the bank] ermöglicht hatten, ein wenig dem Prozess zuwenden, und es war kein Zweifel, dass es gut ausgehen müsste . . . Es gab keine Schuld. Der Prozess war nichts anderes als ein grosses Geschäft, wie er es schon oft mit Vorteil für die Bank abgeschlossen hatte. . .

> . . . das Wohlgefül, endlich einem vernünftigen Menschen [the Inspector] gegenüber zustehen und über seine Angelegenheit mit ihm sprechen zu können, ergriff ihn.

> . . . schein es ihm, als ob durch die Vorfälle des Morgens eine grosse Unordnung in der ganzen Wohnung der Frau Grubach verursacht worden sie und dass gerade er nötig sei, um die Ordnung wiederherzustellen. War aber einmal diese Ordnung hergestellt, dann war jede Spur jener Vorfäll ausgelöscht und alles nahm seinen alten Gang wieder auf.[7]

His delight in bullying people, in playing the petty tyrant, is evident in his relations with Frau Grubach, Fraülein Bürstner, Block, the commercial traveller, and many others. It may be seen too in his encounter with the court of inquiry, in chapter two, when he harangues and forcibly intimidates the judge and the spectators. Intimidation and over-aggressiveness occupy prominent places in his behavior pattern. In addition, K. is characterized by a liking for authority and formality. He is self-important, stubborn, humorless, and calculating, as a close reading of *Der Prozess* will show. All in all he is a rather unpleasant person, a nasty example of the German bourgeoisie.

HOW MEURSAULT DIFFERS FROM JOSEF K.

Meursault is a rather puzzling character, compared to K. We feel that there is something strange, even repellant about him, and yet we sympathize with his choices and actions. From our own knowledge of him, he does not seem to be the

---

7. . . . surely if the abilities which had made this [his high position in the bank] possible were to be applied to the unraveling of his own case, there was no doubt it would go well. . . . There was no guilt. This legal action was nothing more than a business deal such as he had often concluded to the advantage of the Bank. . . .

. . . he was filled with pleasure at having encountered a sensible man [the Inspector] at last, with whom he could discuss the matter.

. . . it seemed to him that the whole household of Frau Grubach had been thrown into great disorder by the events of the morning and that it was his task alone to put it right again. Once order was restored, every trace of these events would be obliterated and things would resume their old course.

"monstre moral"[8] that the prosecutor makes him out to be, and yet exactly what kind of person is he? Sartre thinks he is "un de ces terribles innocents qui font le scandale d'une société parce qu'ils n'acceptent pas les règles de son jue."[9] Camus, himself, says "il est étranger à la société où il vit, il erre, en marge, dans les faubourgs de la vie privée, solitaire, sensuelle."[10] Rhein goes even further:

> Meursault is completely indifferent to everything except physical sensations. . . . He dutifully pursues his profession as a clerk, but he is more interested in the pleasant dryness of a towel in the washroom at mid-day and its clamminess at night than he is in a possible promotion to Paris.

The first thing the reader notices is Meursault's immense apathy. He does not appear to be affected by his mother's death, he is indifferent to marrying Marie and going to Paris, he never seems bothered by the fact that he has killed a man, and he is apparently unconcerned about the outcome of his trial, even though his life is at stake. In addition, he is often bored (witness the way he spends his Sunday), and he is constantly sleepy or sleeping. And who can fail to notice the innumerable occasions when he admits either that he has not been paying attention or that he is unable to follow what is going on? Then there is the fact that he is easily imposed upon (e.g. by Raymond and Salamano), as if his ego-strength were low. Nevertheless, while these personality traits occupy a prominent place in the story, it is easy to exaggerate Meursault's indifference. He is, for example, a rather understanding and sympathetic person (sometimes inappropriately). He readily sympathizes with his employer, Raymond, and Salamano among others. Furthermore, what appears to be indifference is often exhaustion, sleepiness, or mental confusion, as for example at the funeral:

> . . . je lui ai expliqué que j'avais une nature telle que mes besoins physiques dérangeaient souvent mes sentiments. Le jour où j'avais enterré maman, j'étais très fatigué et j'avais sommeil. De sorte que je ne me suis pas rendu compte de ce qui se passait. Ce que je pouvais dire à coup sûr, c'est que j'aurais préféré que maman ne mourût pas.[11]

---

8. "moral monster" 9. "one of those terrible innocents who cause a scandal in a society because they do not accept the rules of its game." 10. He is a foreigner in the society in which he lives; he wanders at the margins, in the outskirts of private, solitary and sensual life." 11. . . . I explained that my physical condition at any given moment often influenced my feelings. For instance, on the day I attended Mother's funeral, I was fagged out and only half awake. So, really, I hardly took stock of what was happening. Anyhow, I could assure him of one thing: that I'd rather Mother hadn't died.

He neglects to mention that it was also extremely hot that day and that too much heat and/or sunlight causes him great physical discomfort, which in turn either makes him sleepy or confuses his mind. It has become a cliché to say that the sun is responsible for the Arab's death, but what is sometimes overlooked is the fact that Meursault's apparent indifference to his trial is largely sleepiness from the great heat. Meursault's love of sensation is easy to exaggerate too. He does, of course, love to swim, sunbathe, and make love to Marie, but he enjoys these things in moderation. It is impossible to picture him as a perpetual thrill-hunter—he simply does not have the energy. "[Raymond] voulait ensuite aller au bordel," he says, "mais j'ai dit non parce que je n'aime pas ça."[12] It would be more correct to say that he was sensation-oriented, that his senses are unusually acute. This explains the towel episode that Rhein mentions and the fact that Meursault often records how things feel, taste, sound, smell, or look.

Perhaps the strangest character trait of all is his concern, indeed his *obsession*, with truth. In situations in which as a matter of convenience the average person would keep quiet or tell a white lie, he goes out of his way to be honest, even volunteering information at times. Thus he tells his lawyer: "Sans doute, j'amais bien maman, mais cela ne voulait rien dire. Tous les êtres sains avaient plus ou moins souhaité la mort de ceux qu'ils aimaient."[13] In all his relations with his lawyer and with the court, he is scrupulously honest. He describes each event and his feelings at the time as exactly as he can, often harming his cause in the process. Similarly, his refusal to weep and crawl before the crucifix-waving judge, or to lament his crime before the prosecutor, eventually costs him his life. In other words, Meursault is martyred because he refuses to falsify his feelings. Camus provides an excellent summary [in "Avant-Propos"]:

> . . . il refuse de mentir. Mentir ce n'est pas seulement dire ce qui n'est pas. C'est aussi surtout, dire plus que ce qui est et, en ce qui concerne le coeur humain, dire plus qu'on ne sent. C'est ce que nous faisons tous, tous les jours, pour simplifier la vie. Il dit ce qu'il est, il refuse de majorer ses sentiments, et aussitôt la société se sent menacée.[14]

12. "After that [Raymond] proposed going to a brothel," he says, "but I refused; I didn't feel like it." 13. "I could truthfully say I'd been quite fond of Mother—but that didn't really mean much. All normal people, I added as an afterthought, had more or less desired the death of those they loved, at some point or another." 14. He refuses to lie. To lie is not only to say what is not true. It is also, above all, to say more than what is true and, as it concerns the human heart, to say more than one feels oneself. It is that which we do all, all the time, to simplify life. He says that which he is; he refuses to raise his sentiments, and forthwith society feels itself menaced.

While the reasons for his total honesty will become evident later, there would seem to be a problem in characterization here. It is difficult to believe that such an indifferent, sleepy, confused individual would care in the least whether he told the truth. Meursault's entire existence is built around the principle of taking the path of least resistance. At stake here is the novel's illusion of realism, which is threatened by this apparently inconsistent behavior.

HOW THE AUTHORS CONSTRUCT THEIR NARRATIVES

While we are discussing characterization, a word or two about narrative devices is in order. The first sentence of *Der Prozess*—"Jemand musste Josef K. verleumdet haben, denn ohne dass er etwas Böses getan hätte, wurde er eines Morgens verhaftet"[15]—gives the impression that Kafka is going to use omniscient narrative. In actuality, however, he relies on a combination of omniscient and third person narrative. This is to say that his omniscience is strictly one-sided. Limited entirely to Josef K., it is not able to penetrate the enigmatic world that surrounds him. The contrast is rather marked—total knowledge versus total ignorance, total intimacy versus total alienation. The narrator (who is never specified) enters K.'s thoughts whenever he wishes and recounts events as if he were looking through K.'s eyes. Thus K. often acts as a sort of filter to the action taking place. Sometimes he tells things just as they happened, other times he alters them slightly for various reasons. Or again, an event may be related objectively by the narrator. This third person narration serves as a check on the omniscient narrative. At the same time it keeps us from getting too close to K., from sympathizing or identifying too much with him. On the whole, Kafka's double focus narrative allows us to form an exceptionally accurate picture of K. We not only become familiar with what and how he thinks, we are able to pull back and observe his interactions with society from a broader perspective.

Camus employs first person narration in *L'Étranger*, but it is a very odd variety, not at all like the usual straight forward narrative. For example, Robert Champigny notes that Meursault refers to an event in both the present and past tenses on the same page:

---

15. "Someone must have traduced Josef K., for without having done anything wrong he was arrested one fine morning.

The "now" of the narrator is mutable. On the first page I read:
"I shall take the bus"; and in the next paragraph, without a
transition: "I took the bus." Further on I read: "today is Saturday"; yet the story of this Saturday is told in the past. The
same shift in tenses occurs in the last chapter.

Often, the past tense seems to refer to the immediate past, as
if the incidents being related had happened recently—earlier
in the day or perhaps a day or two before. There are, for example, several references to "yesterday." But as we continue it
becomes apparent that the story is being told from the *end* of
the series of events of which it is composed, i.e. after all the
events in the novel have taken place. Thus, for instance, we
read: "Alors, j'ai tiré encore quatre fois sur un corps inerte où
les balles s'enfonçaient sans qu'il y parût. Et c'était comme
quatre coups brefs que je frappais sur la porte du malheur." [16]
The last sentence could only have been written (or spoken)
well after Meursault's trial. Perhaps the best way to view the
novel is as a series of year-old entries in a diary which Meursault alternately reads aloud and comments upon. Camus
chooses to tell his story from this point of view because it allows him to look at the whole objectively. With the final events
in mind, Camus—and Meursault—can comment upon the
role of destiny, the "hazard" which plays such an important
part in the book. Like K., Meursault too acts as a sort of filter
to the action taking place, and a certain amount of distortion
is inevitable in spite of his conscientious honesty. In *L'É-
tranger,* as in *Der Prozess,* the narrative technique allows us to
get to know the hero rather thoroughly. In general, because of
the first person narrative, the reader tends to be closer to
Meursault than to K. and to sympathize more with him. None-
theless, like Kafka, Camus wants to keep us from getting too
close to his hero so that we can finally render an objective
judgement. Meursault's apparent indifference, present for
other reasons, serves this purpose admirably.

Before we proceed further, we will need to take a look at
the plots of the two novels, neither one of which is particularly
easy to determine. The difficulty in interpreting *Der Prozess*—
which was never completed—is that everything is fraught
with ambiguity, everything is symbolic. Furthermore. it is difficult to break Kafka's symbolic code because it is not entirely
consistent. Since, as Camus says, symbolism "suppose deux

---

16. "But I fired four shots more into the inert body, on which they left no visible trace.
And each successive shot was another loud, fateful rap on the door of my undoing."

plans, deux mondes d'idées et de sensations, et un diction-naire de correspondance entre l'un et l'autre,"[17] the interpre-tation that explains the greatest number of events and state-ments may be said to be the most valid. Most of the theories that have been proposed have been either theological (meta-physical), psychoanalytical or sociological in nature. In my opinion an existential interpretation, at times hidden behind a Judaeo-Christian metaphor, offers the most satisfactory so-lution. Thus the enigmatic Law, which could theoretically symbolize God's law, is more properly the law of the universe, the law of existence. Similarly, K.'s guilt, which could possibly symbolize original sin, is best interpreted as existential inau-thenticity. K.'s arrest on his thirtieth birthday, the traditional time for taking stock of one's life, symbolizes the beginning of a nagging suspicion that something is wrong with the way he has been living. Throughout the rest of the novel he struggles with this suspicion, trying with less and less success to smother it. However, he steadfastly refuses to admit even the possibility of its validity. Neither Leni, Huld, Titorelli, nor any-one else is able to help him with his (internal) struggle. "Du suchst zuviel fremde Hilfe . . . Merkst du denn nicht, dass es nicht die wahre Hilfe ist?"[18] the prison chaplain asks. But K. refuses to believe him, though of course he should. Then the chaplain relates the parable "Vor dem Gesetz,"[19] the only en-tirely dependable statement about the Law in the whole book. Of course Josef K. misunderstands it: whenever the man from the country asks to enter the Law, the doorkeeper says he can-not admit him at that moment; but finally, when the man is about to die—unadmitted—he learns that the door was in-tended only for him! It should be noted that the parable is a symbolic blueprint, a capsule summary, of the novel. K.'s predicament and his destiny are identical to those of the man from the country. The solutions to their problems are identi-cal too. Instead of waiting passively, the man should have acted, should have vigorously attempted to enter the Law. The same holds true for K. Unknown to him, however, he can only enter the Law by entering into himself. He must learn to act and think in authentic terms.

After chapter nine, "Im Dom,"[20] Kafka intended to describe further stages of the trial but died before he could do so. This

17. "supposes two planes, two worlds of ideas and of feelings, and a dictionary of cor-respondence between the one and the other" 18. "You cast about too much for outside help. . . . Don't you see that it isn't the right kind of help?" 19. "Before the Court" 20. "In the Cathedral"

explains the abrupt shift in action and tone in the final chapter. In chapter ten, K. is markedly changed. Resigned, however, reluctantly to his fate, he is waiting for his executioners when they come. As they walk along, he resists them experimentally, but then Fraülein Bürstner appears (or a woman like her). Her function here is to remind K. of his inherent responsibility, signifying that he should accept the consequences of his actions with dignity. At this point he repents and admits his guilt for the first time, though it comes too late to help him: "Ich wollte immer mit zwanzig Händen in die Welt hineinfahren und uberdies zu einem nicht zu billigenden Zweck. Das war unrichtig." [21] While all he wants at this point is to get it over with, K. deliberately refuses to take his life. His will to live persists. Just before he is executed he gets a tantalizing glimpse of the Law. The windows open on the top story of a house "wie ein Licht aufzuckt" [22]—which recalls the radiance streaming from the door to the Law at the end of the parable—and a figure symbolizing salvation leans forward and stretches out both arms to him. This is clearly a gesture of help, and hope suddenly wells up in him in response. He stretches out both arms to the figure in a gesture of supplication, but at that point he is executed. His death is ugly: "'Wie ein Hund,' sagte er, es war, als sollte die Scham ihn überleben." [23]

THE DUAL PLOT LINES OF *THE STRANGER*

In *L'Étranger* there are actually *two* plot-lines: 1) Meursault's crime and subsequent trial and 2) his metaphysical and philosophical development. It is because Camus relates these two stories simultaneously that he gives us contradictory impressions of Meursault. In order for him to make his point in the first instance, his hero must be scrupulously honest, but his second plot requires that he be apathetic. Countless critics have confused the two plots in trying to give an interpretation consistent with both. Thus Thomas Hanna says:

> The absurdity here is not that of a man in a foreign universe, but in the attempt of society to apply absolute, fixed moral standards in a sphere which has no fixed moral values, human life.

We shall see that in fact *both of* these statements are true.

---

21. "I always wanted to snatch at the world with twenty hands, and not for a very laudable motive, either. That was wrong." 22. "with a flicker as of a light going on" 23. "'Like a dog!' he said; it was as if the shame of it must outlive him."

Regarding the first plot, Meursault is clearly not what the trial makes him out to be. Among other things, he is an accidental rather than an intentional murderer. A close reading of part I, chapter 6, reveals the following: it is by chance that Meursault has Raymond's revolver in his pocket; each time a hot blast of wind or a ray of light hits his eyes he clenches his fist involuntarily; he returns to the stream and the shade only to escape the oppressive sun; he is irrational and nearly unconscious from the sun's effects; when the Arab's knife reflects the sunlight into his eyes, it causes him to clench his fists involuntarily, thus pulling the trigger of the gun he is holding in his coat pocket; at this moment he cannot see the Arab because he is blinded by sweat. Immediately thereafter he shakes off the sweat and the sun and shoots him four more times—why, he never knows. The trial itself requires little comment. Since Meursault admits the murder, the jury has merely to determine whether it was pre-meditated. And since the prosecutor accuses him of being a hardened criminal, a moral monster, what is really on trial is his *entire life.* "Because of his crime," Hanna declares "a clear and absolute judgement must be made on the life of Meursault; an absolute moral criterion must be introduced into his life. . . ." And of course this criterion is bourgeois morality. Meursault's non-conformity to middle class values becomes the basis for his condemnation. By giving the criminal more integrity than the court and jury, Camus is able to launch a devastating attack against the legal process, capital punishment, the middle class, and society in general. Here, then, is the reason for Meursault's great honesty—it is a sign of his inherent integrity.

Camus' second plot, his hero's metaphysical and philosophical development, has greater implications than the first. Virtually all the important developments occur in the last chapter, after he has been condemned to death. In particular, he realizes that he wants very badly to live, to return to that world to which he was once so indifferent. He rejects the consolation that he would die in twenty years anyhow since it is precisely those twenty years that are so precious. When Meursault angrily confronts the chaplain, he discovers what he had always sensed unconsciously—and which seems to have been the source of his apathy—that the world, and everything in it, exists without any justification or purpose: that existence is *absurd.* His immediate reaction is a passionate nihilistic tirade. Then he falls asleep. When he awakes, he feels calm and peaceful. Thinking of his mother, he realizes the *freedom* death gives one and, again, *the importance it gives to life.* These two discoveries provide Meursault with the necessary consciousness and motivation to revolt against the Absurd. At the moment when his life is most in danger, he succeeds in gaining an awareness that will protect him against death. In this manner, he passes from a life of inauthenticity to an authentic existence, however brief. The same process may be observed in *Der Prozess.* . . .

While Kafka's and Camus' social criticism is outside the scope of this study, it is epitomized here in their condemnation of a specific institution: the trial. Though Kafka prefers satire to his colleague's more direct approach, each levels a scathing attack on societal norms. As a Doctor of Jurisprudence himself, the author of *Der Prozess* obviously enjoyed satirizing the absurdities of the legal profession, which in turn mirror the inadequacies of society. This satire, however, does not contribute much to the plot as a whole. After all, the Court is primarily a metaphor here, not a reality. Camus is more successful in integrating his attack on bourgeois justice with his existential plot. However, much we may disapprove of his hero, the judges, lawyers, jurors, and spectators are infinitely more inauthentic. It is not just a question of "lucidity," of existential clarity of thought, though this is obviously important. For Meursault does not attain this state himself until the trial is over. Rather, as Camus remarks elsewhere, what impresses us is his hero's "vérité d'être et de sentir . . . sans laquelle nulle conquête sur soi et sur le monde ne sera jamais possible." [24] This total honesty will greatly aid him in his progress toward existential responsibility. Though Josef K. and Meursault have rather tragic roles to play, *Der Prozess* and *L'Étranger* do not present a pessimistic view of man's fate. The latter is even rather optimistic. Camus chooses to end his story, not with Meursault's nihilistic tirade or with his execution, but on a note of tranquil reflection. Through their failure as individuals, the two heroes offer positive hope to the rest of mankind. In a sense, they are scapegoats who are sacrificed to save the rest of us from the same for-

24. "Truth to be and to feel . . . without that empty conquest over himself and over the world which will never be possible."

tune. Both authors specifically address themselves to the reader and urge him to reflect on the problems that are dramatized in their works. That K. and Meursault are possessed by a strong desire to live at the end underlies their final message: ". . . the infinite value of life lies in the very finiteness of its nature."

CHAPTER 4

Is Meursault to Blame for His Problems?

READINGS ON
THE STRANGER

The Role of Fate in *The Stranger*

Anselm Atkins

The Stranger is often considered as much a work of philosophy as literature. One of the biggest issues in Western philosophy—the relationship between freedom and fate—is central to the perspective brought to the novel by Anselm Atkins, a teacher of literature and theology at the Monastery of the Holy Spirit in Conyers, Georgia. Atkins focuses on the three deaths in the novel and the way in which each of them relates to Meursault's notions about fate and the freedom to act. He argues that Meursault passes through an increasing awareness of death's power to destroy freedom through the death of his mother, the shooting of the Arab and, finally, his own execution.

The dialectic of freedom and fate is a perennial problem in many areas of Western thought. Greek tragedy explored it to its very depths, and contemporary literary criticism continues to make use of its terminology. Christian theology has treated it in the form of the problems of grace and free will, Providence and freedom, and freedom and evil. Even physics deals with a variation of the problem: determinism/indeterminism.

. . . [In *The Stranger*] destiny or fate enters forcefully into the situation of the hero, Meursault. It influences his actions directly, while also appearing indirectly and symbolically as a vague presence. Freedom, too, has its place in Meursault's life.

The obvious starting point for any discussion of fate and freedom is Greek drama. Here the problem originates, and here it achieves its truly classical expression. In interpreting this dialectic, critics and philosophers are often tempted to reduce fate to freedom, or freedom to fate. In the judgement

Excerpted from "Fate and Freedom: Camus's *The Stranger*," by Anselm Atkins, *Renascence: A Critical Journal of Letters*, Winter 1969. Reprinted with permission from *Renascence*.

of [noted Canadian literary critic] Northrop Frye, these two extreme approaches represent limiting cases: the fatalistic reduction, which "exhibits the omnipotence of an external fate," and the moral reduction, which sees tragedy in terms of a (usually morally) wrong choice. Tragedy, Frye insists, seems to require something from both poles. If choice is lacking altogether, the action is ironic rather than tragic: the hero is merely a pitiful victim. But choice, though essential, cannot be the sole determinant in tragic action; it must occur in a context of larger conflicting cosmic forces. [German philosopher] Eric Voegelin, in his *Order and History* has shown that it is precisely the pressure exerted in the hero by two opposed external necessities which gives choice its pivotal role in tragedy. Frye contributes further to the understanding of the interplay of choice and fate by distinguishing the tragic condition and the tragic process. The *tragic process* is a chain of events which the hero sets in motion by a choice. Once started, it cannot be stopped—and therein lies its inevitability. But the hero must have been free to start or not to start it; and this is where freedom enters. The tragic process involves the hero in a loss of freedom, for he is now caught in a tightening web, and he has now his freedom to lose his freedom. He used his freedom to lose his freedom. The archetype of this tragic hero is the Adam depicted by Milton: "sufficient to have stood, yet free to fall." The *tragic condition*, on the other hand, is simply the environment in which man finds himself by the fact of birth. Having been born, he must necessarily die. In this sense, "existence is itself tragic." As modern writers never tire of telling us, man's crime is to have been born.

Camus, unlike Voegelin, does not believe in an objective Order. For him there is no Greek Dike, no divine vendettas, no Christian Providence, and no cosmic teleology of any kind. Consequently, Camus's "fate" cannot be conceived of as a positive ontological force, whether divine, natural, or historical. The cosmic innuendos which the average Westerner hears in the word "fate" are not, strictly speaking, present in Camus's usage. Fate is a negative word implying nothing more than that all men eventually die. Death, then, is the primary antagonist of freedom in Camus's thought. The notion of fate in *The Stranger* can, however, be extended at least metaphorically to all the empirical everyday forces which limit freedom or are symbolically associated with death. In discussing Camus and fate, therefore, the word "fate" should be understood in the larger context of denoting whatever negates freedom. It is the full dialectical opposite of freedom, even though it has no absolute ontological referent.

INESCAPABLE DEATH

The Stranger is structured around three deaths: Meursault's, his mother's, and the Arab's. The story opens with the mother's death, "Mother died today," reaches its climax when Meursault shoots the Arab, and ends with Meursault's death sentence and meditation on death. These three deaths express three phases or degrees of encroachment of fate upon Meursault. The first two deaths prepare the way for the third and last death, his own.

Camus argues in [his 1942 book] *The Myth of Sisyphus* that the inescapability of death voids the very possibility of "ultimate" or metaphysical freedom. Meursault shares this perception. His meditation on the guillotine, an instrument which infallibly kills, shows him the inevitability of death for him personally. Later he comes to the more speculative realization that death is the ultimate canceller of freedom: what a man chooses, how he lives, what he has done, all make no difference, since the one same fate—death—chooses all alike. Death is the "slow persistent breeze" blowing towards one all during life. Death, then, in removing Meursault from the world, removes also the last vestige of his freedom. His impending execution at the end of the novel brings the final victory of fate over his freedom.

The death of Meursault's mother marks the first stage in the development of the situation in which fate gradually overshadows his freedom. Her death is the first large intrusion of fate into his life, the first narrowing down of freedom in a process which gains momentum until it reaches the point where the narrowing will be complete. His mother's death is itself a harbinger of fate in several ways. It is, first of all, an external pressure: Meursault did not choose it, and, as he says later, he would have preferred that she had not died. Going to Marengo on the bus is an unwanted inconvenience. There is no question of his not attending the funeral; convention constrains him. As if to emphasize the pressures which make him go, he three times remarks that the funeral was "not his fault." More important, his going to the funeral initiates a series of actions on his part which will later be held against him at the trial and actually constitute the cause of his conviction and death. Thus his mother's death, which breaks in on him from the outside, pushes him along one of those innocent paths which may—and in this case did—lead to prison.

The murder of the Arab—the second death in the chain—tightens the grip of fate. Its immediate effect is Meursault's confinement in prison, where he becomes aware of his loss of liberty to come and go. He knows that his cell is a "dead end." He has to give up the habit of "thinking like a free man." The worst punishment of jail is his "being deprived of liberty." He can no longer smoke, swim, or see Marie (except at the visitors' grill). The chafing restrictions drive him to grasp at surrogates for freedom. Having no female companionship, he takes the jailer's hint and begins masturbating. A second substitute is memory, which he now cultivates extensively. Meursault knows that this impingement of fate on his freedom is due to his murder of the Arab: "With that crisp, whipcrack sound, it all began. . . . And each successive shot was another loud, fateful rap on the door of my undoing." His description here is, of course, in retrospect; but even at the time of the murder he knew that he had "shattered the balance of the day." And the balance he shattered was the delicate balance between freedom and fate which Frye calls "the balancing condition of life"—broken when a violation of "justice" in the "tragic condition" launches the inexorable "tragic process." Plainly, then, Meursault's murder starts a chain of causes which will eventually obliterate his freedom.

THE SYMBOLS OF FATE

The sun and the sea are constant motifs in Camus's writings. [American critic] Carl Viggiani has shown in a skillful Freudian study how these two symbols attract other things into their orbits to form symbol-clusters with uniform meanings. To the sun-symbol are annexed the father and other authority figures: judges, obnoxious old men, priests, policemen, even God. The sun thus comes to symbolize any external repressive force which lessens freedom. The sun, of course, also symbolizes other things for Camus—life and warmth, for instance. In *The Stranger,* however . . . the sun is nearly always oppressive. This is particularly true at the crucial moments when fate intrudes into Meursault's life: at

ABSURD FREEDOM

In his discussion of the fate in The Stranger, *Anselm Atkins repeatedly refers to Camus's first major philosophical work* The Myth of Sisyphus. *Published in the same year as* The Stranger, *this work treats a number of the same concepts as the novel, albeit in non-fictional form. The excerpt from this work that appears below outlines Camus's ideas about the limits of human ability to make meaning out of the larger world. Note the similarities between Camus's statements here and those expressed by Meursault in the chapters after his trial.*

History is not lacking in either religions or prophets, even without gods. He is asked to leap. All he can reply is that he doesn't fully understand, that it is not obvious. Indeed, he does not want to do anything but what he fully understands. He is assured that this is the sin of pride, but he does not understand the notion of sin; that perhaps hell is in store, but he has not enough imagination to visualize that strange future; that he is losing immortal life, but that seems to him an idle consideration. An attempt is made to get him to admit his guilt. He feels innocent. To tell the truth, that is all he feels— his irreparable innocence. This is what allows him everything. Hence, what he demands of himself is to live *solely* with what he knows, to accommodate himself to what is, and to bring in nothing that is not certain. He is told that nothing is. But this at least is a certainty. And it is with this that he is concerned: he wants to find out if it is possible to live *without appeal.*

Excerpted from Albert Camus, *The Myth of Sisyphus and Other Essays* (translated by Justin O'Brien). New York: Alfred A. Knopf, 1967, pp. 51–53.

the funeral, on the beach, and in the courtroom during the trial which determines his death sentence.

The sun not only stands over the action as a hostile presence, but even enters into it. It contributes actively to the murder. Meursault, walking on the beach, is driven by its heat to seek relief in the shade of a rock—the rock by which the Arab is sitting. Meursault keeps going toward the rock in spite of the threat presented by the Arab: "The whole beach, pulsing with heat, was pressing on my back. I took some steps toward the stream [by the rock]." He advances further: "I couldn't stand [the heat] any longer, and took another step forward." At the trial he sums up the incident with the laconic remark that he killed the Arab "because of the sun." The sun is in great measure the principal in the murder, and

Meursault merely its instrument. Is it a coincidence that Apollo (whose oracle the fated Oedipus fulfilled) was the god of the sun? Like Oedipus, Meursault is driven to his unlucky end by solar powers.

The wind symbolizes fate too. The "slow, persistent breeze" of death which Meursault says has been blowing toward him all his life is, like the sun, a real agent at one point in the narrative. As he watched the Arab's glinting knife, "everything began to reel before my eyes, a fiery gust came from the sea, while the sky cracked in two, from end to end, and a great sheet of flame poured down through the rift." The wind, the "fiery gust," is only one of the atmospheric forces bearing down on him at this critical moment. Just as at his mother's funeral, there is "something inhuman" about the very landscape. The clashing "cymbals of the sun" reduplicate in heightened form the throbbing of the air at the funeral. The wind that nudges him toward murder is the same inhuman cosmic breeze—death—which levels the value of all choices by reducing them to the last stillness of the grave.

The wall, symbol of the "inescapability of death," occurs in only one episode in *The Stranger*, but its sense is clear. The last chapter of the book (in which the wall figures) shows a significant increase in the use of words indicative of restriction and spatial limitation. Because the stone walls of Meursault's prison cell are so omnipresent and solid, they are a stark symbol of restriction. Both he and the priest lean on them. For the priest they betoken human suffering—but they also seem to represent the will of God, whose face the priest supposes all prisoners see taking shape on them. For Meursault, since God is absent, the grey walls would suggest not a personal ordering force in the universe, but rather a senseless fate herding men toward death. Much as he tries, he cannot even see Marie's face there. Finally, Camus uses "walls" in *The Myth of Sisyphus* as one of the obvious symbols of the absurd: "All man has is his lucidity and his definite knowledge of the walls surrounding him." Just as man cannot fathom the absurd universe, so he cannot extend his freedom beyond the blank wall of death. Death is the hardest prison wall, the last trick of fate.

Ignorance, Chance, and Fate

Fate, one may conclude, enters significantly into the structure and symbolism of the novel. But it is prominent also in

Meursault's mental life. His sense of an overhanging fate is strongest, naturally enough, in the last chapter. "The only thing that interests me now is the problem of circumventing the machine, learning if the inevitable admits a loophole." He speaks of "the implacable machinery of justice," the "wheels" in "that inexorable march of events" leading to certain death under the guillotine. What bothers him about the guillotine is its mechanical perfection. He does not have even a gambler's chance: "I was caught in the rat trap irrevocably." These expressions are wholly appropriate to the workings of fate, which is the wheel of fortune, the fine-grinding mill of the gods, the cosmic machine. He seems to hint at fate when, in his tirade to the priest, he says that the certainty of death "had got its teeth into me." The way a man decides to live his life makes no difference because the same fate—death—"chooses" him and every other man. An earlier scene emphasizes the same point. While Meursault is in prison prior to the trial, he recalls, as he stands at his barred window, a remark passed by the nurse at the funeral: "If you go too slowly there's risk of a heatstroke. But, if you go too fast, you perspire, and the cold air in the church gives you a chill." "I saw her point," he had said; "either way one was in for it." There is no escaping fate. And that was Oedipus's predicament: he would have been caught by Apollo's oracle no matter what he had done to avoid it. By fleeing Corinth to get away from it, he ran directly into it. "No," Meursault reflects, "there is no way out."

The notion of ignorance as an ingredient of unfreedom helps to illumine the general relationship of Part I of the novel to Part II. Since the evidence presented in the farcical trial in Part I gives wholly unforeseen meanings to Meursault's actions in Part I, those actions take on an aspect of having been committed in partial ignorance. Now ignorance has always been regarded as a limitation on freedom and responsibility. One cannot help feeling that Oedipus's ignorance of his own and his parents' identity decreases his guilt and makes his crimes specifically different from true parricide and incest. So also in *The Stranger:* Meursault had no way of knowing the twisted yet fatal interpretation which would later be put upon his casual acts. He plunged on—as indeed we all do—without full knowledge of the consequences. In the here and now such acts are free; but in retrospect they appear as blind stitches in an unexpected and unwilled pattern. They fit into a picture not envisioned by the painter.

. . . Chance, too, like ignorance, is a contributor to unfreedom. Chance is the apparently uncaused convergence of two or more lines of causality. The lines themselves are fully determined and causally explicable, but their crossing is not. The crossing is outside man's choosing, planning, or understanding, and falls schematically in the domain of fate. To be sure, one ordinarily thinks of fate as that which is fixed, and of chance as that which is only too unfixed. The indeterminate character of chance happenings might make them look like allies of freedom; but since chance robs man of purposive control over his life, it must in the present context be taken as an enemy of freedom. . . . Meursault's life is certainly influenced by chance. At the trial the Prosecutor asks him why he had taken a revolver and returned to the place where the Arab had been encountered earlier. He replies (truthfully, one must suppose), "it was a matter of pure chance." His friend Céleste says of the murder, "it was just an accident, or a stroke of bad luck," and is "flabbergasted" when the Judge utterly disregards his testimony. Marie, in her turn, tells of her swim with Meursault, the film, and their liaison. The Prosecutor sees in these actions not chance but evidence of Meursault's sinister character and evil motivation. (Since there is no doubt that Meursault committed the killing, the question at issue is the nature of his interior disposition.) But it seems rather clear that Marie is right in feeling that the Prosecutor has gotten the motivation "all wrong." For those acts of Meursault, though essentially free, were not performed with a high degree of awareness. As free acts they were limited from two points of view: they are not done with full knowledge of their consequences, and they are fortuitous as far as Meursault is concerned.

A perfect example of chance—the uncaused convergence of unconnected lines of causality—is Meursault's meeting with Marie in the swimming pool. He chose to go to the pool, but he did not choose Marie's being there. As for his consent to attend the Fernandel film and his subsequent affair with Marie, he is indeed responsible—and here the freedom which he does exercise is exemplified; but one must not forget that she cooperated fully, and was the one who first wanted to see the Fernandel film. Lastly, the shooting of the Arab is described as being accidental. Meursault is in an extremely tense state: "Every nerve in my body was a steel spring, and my grip closed on the revolver. The trigger gave . . ." From this brief account it seems that he did not intend to pull the trigger at all; the contrary is at least strongly suggested. What Meursault and Céleste say at the trial is, therefore, very largely true; the murder was an accident.

It is in the context of fate that one should understand Meursault's strange fascination with the newspaper clipping about the murdered Czech, a story he reread "thousands of times." Why did Camus insert this story into his carefully constructed novel? Why does it come where it does—and what does Meursault see in it? One might be inclined to think that he identifies himself with the murdered son by virtue of their mistaken identity. For Meursault is manifestly misunderstood by the court. The judge and jury never comprehend his true inner character. Like the son in the clipping who concealed his true name from his mother, Meursault also seems at times (though not, to be sure, always) unnecessarily reticent about himself. But this explanation will not work, because Meursault recounts the story of the Czech *before* the trial—and it is only during the trial that he learns that his "identity" has been mistaken. Nor can the mother be a link, for Meursault does not yet know that his conviction will hinge on his cool behavior toward her at the funeral. Other grounds must be provided if the story is to be connected with the plot and content of the novel. Fortunately, Camus's [1944] play *The Misunderstanding,* which is modeled on the Czech murder case, provides the answer. In this expanded version of the murder one can see that Camus regarded it an instance of the workings of fate. In the play Jan, the murdered son, enters his mother's inn but is not recognized by her. So surprised is he by this that he jestingly assumes a false name, and then decides to "let things take their course." This occurrence, he later tells his wife, was simply "the force of things." Again, while the mother is sitting beside the drugged son wondering whether or not to go on with the murder, she says, "he is living through a moment when he has no say in his fate; when his hopes of life are made over to indifferent hands." How very like the indifferent and fatalistic universe to which Meursault resigns himself in the final prison scene! After the murder when the mother's announced suicide shatters her daughter's hopes for a new life at the seaside, the mother answers, "it only proves that in a world where everything can be denied, there are forces undeniable." Like Meursault, the mother "ruined everything" by one act: "I have lost my freedom and my hell has just begun." The daughter, too, agrees that "everything happened as it was bound to happen"—which is equivalent, she feels, to saying that "this world doesn't make sense." She is convinced that what "happened was not an accident"—that is, it was bound to happen. (It is in this light that one mug interpret her earlier assertion that "chance doesn't enter into it" when one murders travelers.) She talks like a woman in a foredoomed world in which fate has entirely shut out freedom. The story, then, is essentially one of fate. Since, therefore, Meursault tells the story of the Czech while he is bemoaning his own loss of freedom, and since it is clear from the above analysis that Camus, in the expanded version, sees the Czech murder case as an example of the action of fate, it is only natural to see its appearance at just this point in *The Stranger* as another reference to fate.

MEURSAULT'S FREEDOM(S)

. . . Meursault is a lucid absurd man in his last days, and evidently enjoys "freedom of attitude," inner freedom. His tirade against the priest and his brief concluding meditation leave no room for doubt. He denies the priest's God, says that the only certainty is death and that no action is more meaningful or valuable than any other. In the meditation he likens his condition to his mother's: "on the brink of freedom, ready to start life all over again." Cornered by death, emptied of hope, he feels himself most free. "For the first time," he says, "I laid my heart open to the benign indifference of the universe." He fits exactly the description in *The Myth of Sisyphus* of the man who has the "bottomless certainty" of death, the sense of "liberation," and the "divine availability of the condemned man before whom the prison doors open in a certain early dawn, that unbelievable disinterestedness with regard to everything except the pure flame of life, . . . the only reasonable freedom."

A more difficult question is whether Meursault has been lucid and absurd throughout his whole life. The question is not merely academic, since the answer to it will affect one's verdict on the extent of his "freedom of attitude." As far as one can tell, the first time he self-consciously formulates his position as an absurd man is in the closing scene described above. But he has acted like an absurd man long before. When he declines his boss's offer of a better job in Paris, for example, he shows the lack of ambition which characterizes the man who is not the slave of purposes. When he refuses to treat Marie's marriage proposal seriously he is like the absurd man for whom it makes no difference "how a man decides to live." The disinterestedness and remoteness from life which, according to *The Myth of Sisyphus*, accompany the absurd man's freedom of attitude, are perhaps the most striking features of Meursault's so-called "alienation." And his "freedom with regard to common rules" (social conventions) at his mother's funeral and frequently thereafter is what he is eventually condemned for. That his freedom is indeed from "common rules" is also suggested by [the essay] "Summer In Algiers," where Camus mentions some of the few rules the absurd man *does* observe. Virtue is meaningless for the Algerians, but they—like Hemingway's heroes—have their "code." For instance, "you don't double up on an adversary, because 'that looks bad.'" Meursault and his two companions, Raymond and Masson, follow this part of the code to the letter: they pair off against the two Arabs, leaving the extra man (Meursault) on the sidelines as a lookout. Meursault, then, even before his illumination, shows traits of the absurd man. And to these traits could be added many other. But one passage in *The Stranger* is particularly convincing. "I'd been right," he tells the priest at the end, "I was still right, I was always right. I'd passed my life in a certain way, and I might have passed it in a different way, if I'd felt like it. . . . And what did that mean? That, all the time, I'd been waiting for this present moment, for that dawn, tomorrow's or another day's, which was to justify me." Meursault's life is a unity—lucidly absurd from beginning to end. His last hours differ from his earlier years only in being more articulate. He has the absurd man's freedom of attitude—certainly at his death, and probably long before.

"Freedom of action"—the garden-variety of freedom—is what Camus refers to when he says "I can experience only my own freedom" (as opposed to metaphysical freedom). It is the ordinary ability to choose and determine courses of action in everyday life: the freedom "which the human heart can experience and live." It implies a lack of external restraint, and might best be indicated in *The Stranger* as that type of freedom which Meursault loses—and misses so

keenly—when he goes to prison. The absurd man has, a sur-
plus of this freedom, for his "freedom of attitude" removes
many of the artificial restraints which bind the man entan-
gled in conventional values and purposes.

How much freedom of action does Meursault have? Fate,
as was shown earlier, has a heavy-handed way with him.
His freedom is what is left over after fate has taken its share.
Metaphysical freedom, of course, is non-existent for him. He
does, on the other hand, have freedom of attitude. But it is
hard to tell at first glance whether he has any freedom of action. For the forces of fate in the novel, especially the three
deaths and their effects, gradually erase any freedom of this
type which he may have had. Some critics, in fact, think
Meursault never has any freedom at all. According to [Amer-
ican literary critic Murray] Krieger, he refuses to make
choices, is totally passive and indifferent, and is led by whim
and caprice or pushed around like an automaton. "All is
fated," and "in declining to play a conscious role, [Meur-
sault] turns his strings over at Pattern, which finds his way
for him." What Krieger says is largely true and brings out the
fatalistic aura of the book. But his view is a little one-sided.
As has already been shown, Meursault, in prison, grieves
over the loss of something which he therefore must once
have possessed—namely, a kind of freedom which tallies
with the "freedom of action" described in *The Myth of Sisyphus*. One can see that some of his actions were at least
partly free: his decision to go swimming and his consent to
accompany Marie to the Fernandel film. And there are other
holes in the net of his fate which must be taken into account.

In establishing criteria for evidences of Meursault's freedom of action, one is scarcely justified in demanding instances of tense, dramatic, soul-searching decisions. Until
Meursault kills the Arab, his life is unmomentous, unheroic,
rather uninteresting, and played on a very low scale. And the
style of the book perfectly matches the hero's drab stature.
As nearly every critic has observed, the language is subdued
almost to the point of flatness. The critic has only nuances
and meager indications to guide him, and must be content
with what Camus chooses to furnish. Meursault is a low-
mimetic hero, and neither his freedom nor his unfreedom is
discernable as long as one looks only for highly charged
conflict and heroic posing. If this methodological postulate
is accepted, a great deal of slender-looking evidence be-

comes available for showing that Meursault is really free. His choices are not conspicuous, but they are there, and in sufficient number to be a consistent feature of Meursault's character. To judge by his actions, he is as free as any man.

... The clearest case of Meursault's freedom of action comes at the climax of the book. The ingredients of fate which influenced his shooting of the Arab have already been explained: the comic forces of hot wind and sun, the strong attraction of the cool shade of the rock, and the possibly accidental nature of the trigger-pulling itself. Yet he is not altogether coerced. A free choice plays a vital part in the deed considered as a whole. Aware of the danger ("I gripped Raymond's revolver"), Meursault approaches the Arab. "It struck me," he remember, "that all I had to do was to turn, walk away, and think no more about it" He felt that he was being pressed forward by the heat—yet he could have turned back, and he knew it. His fatal choice at this point was a free one.

The relationship between fate and freedom which comes to light in *The Stranger* corresponds closely with that underlying Greek tragedy. Viggiani is right . . . in insisting that Meursault's "career, in its understated, plebeian way is patterned after that of tragic heroes of antiquity"; that is, it is partly free. How, after all, do fate and freedom work in Greek tragedy? In *Oedipus Tyrannus,* on the side of fate, there is the fulfillment of Apollo's oracle. What was predicted happens. Chance and choice pile together until the sum of chances and choices becomes—the inevitable. In spite of the predetermined outcome, however, Oedipus is not an automaton. He has the liberty of spontaneous self-direction, or what most philosophers would call free choice (or what Camus would call "freedom of action"). Time after time, both on stage and in the offstage prehistory, Oedipus makes rational decisions. If he is in a double sense innocent—innocent through ignorance and innocent at the hands of fate—he is nevertheless in another sense guilty: as guilty as any man who freely kills another man at a crossroads. Oedipus, however, though free, is not free to escape his destiny. He moves, but within a cage. He moves freely, but toward a fate not of his choosing. His destiny is an over-arching canopy sealed tight at the edges. His freedom may run its little course along the earth, but it will always meet the iron rim of heaven at the horizon. Fate and freedom maintain themselves, in classical tragedy, in a delicate balance. This tragic balance of fate and freedom recurs in all its complexity in *The Stranger.*

Meursault's Passivity Leads to His Death

Germaine Brée

Germaine Brée, professor of philosophy at New York University, was both a contemporary and an acquaintance of Camus. The 1959 book from which this excerpt was taken was one of the earliest large-scale studies of Camus's work. Brée argues that Meursault is initially presented as a character who does not question any aspect of his own existence. She cites this behavior as the reason that Meursault commits the murder that eventually leads to his own death. Nevertheless, once Meursault has reflected upon the meaning of his life, he can reconcile himself to something of a "happy" death. Not only this, but he also serves as a warning to the reader not to simply exist passively and risk making the same sort of mistake.

Meursault, the hero of *The Stranger*, is a kind of Adam, a man content just to live and who asks no questions. But like Melville's Billy Budd, Meursault kills a man. He is then judged to be guilty, but why? The prosecutor, lawyer, and chaplain answer the question in conventional semi-social, semi-religious, Occidental terms, but these officials represent abstract entities and their answers mean nothing to Meursault nor to a simple-minded man like Meursault's friend, Céleste; quite obviously their explanations do not apply to the case as Camus devised it.

But as the tale develops it seems clear that Meursault's error lies precisely in his estrangement. He acts in a human situation as though human relationships, and therefore responsibilities, do not exist, and before he knows it he is involved in Raymond's elementary but violent drama. That Meursault killed the Arab is a fact. That his act was not premeditated and that there was provocation is also a fact. But at the trial what both prosecution and defense present to the jury are all the unrelated events in Meursault's life between his mother's death and the murder; these events are presented in a logically organized whole as the basis of an interpretation of Meursault's personality. As Meursault sits in bewildered surprise through this reconstruction of his crime, he begins to feel that he is being condemned to death because he was found guilty of not crying at his mother's funeral. And in a sense he is right. In fact he is condemned, according to Camus himself, "because he does not play the game." He is a stranger to society, because he refuses to make any concession whatsoever to its codes and rituals. He sees no relation at all between his mother's death and the fact that he goes to see a comic film two days later, and he establishes none. And, seeing through his eyes, we are almost in complete agreement with him. He is, as Camus himself has said, the man who refuses to lie.

Meursault's attitude at first merely reveals how arbitrary and superficial are the codes with which we cover up the stark incomprehensibility of life; for example, we can feel it is enough, in the presence of death, if we simply refrain from smoking a cigarette. With a certain fierce humor Camus uses his hero to shake us out of our complacency and to ridicule our smugness. But when Meursault goes even further, refusing to humor the prosecutor's Christian pathos because he sees no relation between his own act and the crucifix, refusing to take the "leads" of his lawyer, which play on a stock set of conventional emotional values, he becomes a kind of social martyr, a man who "dies rather than lie" in answer to a question. It is not, however, the satire of a society and the miscarriage of justice that give the tale its fundamental significance. With the shooting of the Arab, Meursault tells us, "everything began," and more specifically still, "everything began" in the prison after Marie's one and only visit, "everything," that is Meursault's inner transformation.

THE DIFFERENT STAGES OF MEURSAULT'S LIFE

Once or twice in the course of the tale we catch a glimpse of an earlier Meursault, for example the student who had once been to Paris: presumably he had not always lived in the passive, autonomous state in which we find him. In this respect his precursor, Patrice (*A Happy Death*), gives us an excellent clue to Meursault's adventure which, like his own, is essentially spiritual in nature. At one stage in his spiritual career Patrice had aspired to become similar to an object, to live timelessly and to be one with the world. Meursault seems to have achieved this state at the beginning of *The Stranger.* "Meursault, for me," writes Camus, is "a poor and naked man, in love with the sun which leaves no shadows. He is far from being totally deprived of sensitivity for he is animated by a passion, profound because it is tacit, the passion for the absolute and for truth. It is still a negative truth, the truth of being and feeling, but a truth without which no conquest of the self or of the world is possible." That is why, until the very end, Meursault is the man who answers but never asks a question, and all his answers alarm a society which cannot bear to look at the truth.

But the revolver shot jolts Meursault out of his purely negative state. At the time he is aware that he has committed an irreparable act: "I understood that I had destroyed the equilibrium of the day, the unusual silence of a beach where I had been happy." As in the case of Dimitri Karamazov, [in Dostoyevsky's *The Brothers Karamazov*] the real crime is not the one for which Meursault is being tried, but another which he will understand fully at the end when he accedes to a new level of awareness, conquering the world and himself as he grasps the nature of that happiness of which he had had a vague premonition on the beach.

Immediately after his imprisonment, Meursault—like Patrice in Prague after the murder of Zagreus—plunges into a new timeless world, the endless, uniform prison day. There he discovers three inexhaustible but completely closed subjective worlds: the world of memory; the world of sleep; and, as he scans over and over again a newspaper item (a murder story), the world of human solitude. Thus he "kills time," living, as it were, a timeless existence, but an existence which brings him only apathetic sadness. To him in his prison, his face is now that of a stranger, an exile.

The final revelation comes like a flash just before Meursault's death. In spite of Meursault, the prison chaplain has come to speak of forgiveness, of an after-life in which all may be redeemed. For the first time since he shot the Arab Meursault is jolted out of his apathy and in an access of rage he violently shakes the priest. There is no after-life. There is only one life, his life as he knew it—the swims and the beaches, the evenings and Marie's light dresses and soft body—an intense, glorious life that needs no redeeming, no regrets, no tears. Why cry at his mother's funeral? Why lament his own death? After all he is no different from any other human being: all are condemned to death just as he is, except that he knows both the glory of life and the unjustifiable nature of death. His crime and his revelation are as one. He destroyed and is destroyed. For this destruction there is no explanation, excuse, or compensation. The anguished hours of self-torture in his prison cell are over; he no longer calculates endlessly how he may escape. Defiant and lucid, he will go to his death happy:

> As if my great outburst of anger had purged me of evil, emptied now of all hope, face to face with a night heavy with signs and stars, I abandoned myself to the tender indifference of the world. Feeling it . . . so fraternal at last, I knew I had been happy, and that I was still happy. So that all might be consummated, so that I might feel less alone, all that was left for me to wish was that there should be many spectators the day of my execution and that they should greet me with cries of hatred.

Meursault here becomes a sacrificial victim, his end is an apotheosis [elevation to divine status], the equivalent of Patrice's "happy death," a descent into the sea and sun, a reintegration into the cosmos. The stranger has in his prison cell, on the brink of death, found his kingdom: the irreplaceable every-moment life of an ordinary human being who by an inexplicable decree of fate is destined to death. Meursault, as Camus conceived him, must disappear with this revelation.

It is clear that Meursault's initial mental attitude proves inadequate to cope with even the simplest of lives. The very essence of *l'absurde* in his case is that out of indifference he linked forces with violence and death, not with love and life. Like Parsifal in the legend of the Fisher-King he fails to ask any question and thereby gravely errs. In *The Stranger* Camus thus suggests that in the face of the absurd no man can afford passively just to exist. To fail to question the meaning of the spectacle of life is to condemn both ourselves, as individuals, and the whole world to nothingness.

Meursault Seeks His Own Punishment

C. Roland Wagner

Meursault's supposed indifference to the world around him is a characteristic that numerous critics have focused on in their analyses of *The Stranger*. C. Roland Wagner, professor of Humanities at Hofstra University, departs somewhat from the mainstream in his perspective on this element of the story. Wagner claims that Meursault's seeming indifference—represented by his silence in certain important situations— is the product of feelings within Meursault that he consciously or unconsciously fails to address. The most important of these for Wagner is Meursault's wish to be reunited with his dead mother. Meursault's silence represents psychological instability that actually is contrary to what Camus intends Meursault to represent. Wagner, unlike most critics, claims that the novel fails because Meursault's unacknowledged feelings ultimately prevent him from reaching the kind of understanding that Camus wishes to attribute to him.

How to prove that the "indifferent" Meursault really collaborates in his own downfall? We need not go far to show that beneath his calm surface Meursault is not altogether indifferent, that he is even a man of intense, if severely concentrated passions. Camus himself, we have seen, speaks of his "passion for the absolute and for truth." (In *The Myth of Sisyphus* Camus declares that the courageous man lives joyfully in the "absurd" confrontation between his quest for the absolute—a "nostalgia for unity"—and the hard truth of a universe in which that quest must fail.) Certainly Meursault's hidden "passion for truth" becomes completely visible in the exultant peroration with which the novel ends: "I laid my heart open to the benign indifference of the universe". But where in the text are the verbal or behavioral correlatives to his "passion for the absolute"? Sartre, in his explication of *The Stranger*, remarks that Meursault is a not altogether satisfactory absurdist hero because he apparently does not possess "that hidden gnawing . . . which is due to the blinding presence of death." And this is not an unusual reading of the novel. But if we link the philosophical or conceptual meaning of the absolute to its psychological or experiential meaning, I think we can find a basis for Camus's claim. I don't know if Camus clearly intended it, but Meursault's unverbalized, semi-conscious feeling for his mother—a feeling that *is* clearly pointed up in the novel—works *novelistically* as the equivalent of that philosophical "passion for the absolute." The longing for maternal unity, the infra-rational desire to be reunited with the departed Mother, is, for Meursault, the sensory equivalent of the supra-rational dream of philosophical unity. It is *his* quest for a satisfaction that cannot be attained in this world.

But Meursault's hidden yearning is not revealed in so many words. It is adumbrated through the technique of parallel structures. How he really feels about his mother can be deduced by examining Meursault's underground link with the love and love-hate relationships of others in the novel. Old Salamano and his dog, Raymond and his Arab mistress, an Arab prisoner and his mother, all have unexpressed meaning for the hero; they tell us more about him than he can tell us himself. Salamano, for example, who (like Raymond, the pimp) lives on the same floor of the dank apartment house as Meursault, has mistreated his ugly, mangy dog for years until, finally, the terrorized animal runs away and leaves Salamano without a companion. Meursault listens to the "little wheezing sound" of the old man weeping next door: "For some reason, I don't know what, I began thinking of Mother. But I had to get up early next day; so, as I wasn't feeling hungry, I did without supper, and went straight to bed." The fact that at this moment he "wasn't feeling hungry" is not in itself important, but if we remember that at the all night vigil for his dead mother at the Home for Aged Persons the supposedly indifferent Meursault also "wasn't hungry" and skipped his dinner, both instances of not eating may reinforce one another—both may express a half-buried emotional attachment. (It is easy to forget Meursault's lack of appetite at the vigil because later so much is made of the fact that he drank *café au lait* and smoked cigarettes.)

Another less direct suggestion of unexpressed feeling may be found in an earlier passage, before the dog is lost, when Meursault stands on his landing—he describes the building as "quiet as the grave," reminding us of the mother's death—hearing "nothing but the blood throbbing in [his] ears . . . Then the dog began to moan in old Salamano's room, and through the sleep-bound house the little plaintive sound rose slowly, like a flower growing out of the silence and the darkness." Interestingly, Camus eliminated the last clause (a separate sentence in the French), beginning with "through the sleepbound house . . . ," in the final edition of *The Stranger*. Perhaps he thought that the image was too extreme and too early—too early in the novel before the climax of the murder—a violation of Meursault's simple, relatively non-metaphysical style. But it may also have been because it suggests too forcefully a depth of emotion that Meursault might feel but could not be conscious of. Yet the image is in keeping with the silence between mother and son, and the intense, inaudible love that grew in that silence.

A final suggestion occurs later, when Meursault is in prison and Marie comes to visit him for the first and last time. She faces him across a gap of about thirty feet, and both of them are behind high iron grilles, through which the prisoners and visitors talk to each other. Here the parallel structure is provided by an Arab prisoner, squatting next to Meursault, whose visitor is a "small old woman with tight-set lips," squatting next to Marie. ". . . The prisoner on my left, a youngster with thin, girlish hands, never said a word. His eyes, I noticed, were fixed on the little old woman opposite him, and she returned his gaze with a sort of hungry passion." In the midst of all the noise of prisoners and visitors talking to one another, the "only oasis of silence was made by the young fellow and the old woman gazing into each other's eyes."

MEURSAULT'S INDIFFERENT RESPONSE TO HIS MOTHER'S INDIFFERENCE

Once we have struck through the mask of indifference, Camus's parallel structures help us to find other unexpressed, but more deeply unconscious feelings in Meursault besides intense love for his mother. At this point, however, we are moving into difficult terrain, for we are, I think, going well beyond the author's intent, and even contradicting his purposes in *The Stranger*. For if, as I shall maintain, the novel at its profoundest implies that Meursault is ambivalent and guilt-ridden where his mother is concerned, the work itself denies Camus's own conception of his hero as the "innocent" victim of society's aggression. As we have already noted, although Camus saw him as limited, perhaps as excessively passive, he did not see him as evil, murderous or sub-human. He did not see him as secretly committed to the events in which he is caught up. But the novel itself, when read psychoanalytically, tells otherwise. Hence the special need for a psychoanalytical approach to this puzzling work.

Is it not likely that if Meursault must hide his strong feelings for his mother he is hiding other feelings as well? His inability to recognize the intensity of his love is itself the clue to more profound repressions. Let me offer the hypothesis that his indifference is his defense against maternal rejection, a defense against his mother's apparent indifference to him. ("'. . . For years she'd never had a word to say to me, and I could see she was moping, with no one to talk to.'") The hatred and the guilt locked inside that indifference eventually lead Meursault to send his mother away, whereupon the guilt increases; and at her death everything comes to a boil.

Chapters III and IV are crucial for verifying this hypothesis, or at least for making it plausible. The events that lead to the murder begin here with Meursault's decision to involve himself in Raymond's plans for revenge on his Arab mistress (whom Raymond suspects of infidelity). The word "decision" may seem inappropriate to describe Meursault's mental processes: the strange reason he gives for writing a letter to help Raymond prepare the girl for her "punishment" is that he "wanted to satisfy Raymond, as I'd no reason not to satisfy him." But unconsciously the decision is a real one, I think, for it expresses Meursault's ambivalent attitude towards his mother. As Raymond felt "let down" by his mistress, Meursault felt let down by his mother's failure to respond the way he wished. He sees in Raymond's sadistic treatment of the girl the appropriate response of the rejected suitor: "I told him one could never be quite sure how to act in such cases, but I quite understood his wanting her to suffer for it." Of course this can be read in a perfectly innocent way, but it makes sense to keep the unconscious dimension in mind and to recognize that more than merely objective understanding may be implied here.

"May" verges on "must" the following Sunday. Three things are happening at about the same time on Meursault's landing: Salamano is mistreating his dog as they go out for a walk ("'Filthy brute! Get on, you cur!'"); Meursault and his girl friend Marie, having slept together the previous night, are getting their lunch ready ("When she laughed I wanted her again. A moment later she asked me if I loved her. I said that sort of question had no meaning, really; but I supposed I didn't."); Raymond is beating and yelling at his mistress ("'You let me down, you bitch! I'll learn you to let me down!'"). Meursault's unconscious life is being expressed by both Salamano and Raymond, and we understand why he is unable to commit himself to Marie. Although Marie is amused by Salamano she is horrified by Raymond's behavior and asks Meursault to get a policeman. He refuses, because he "didn't like policemen," but one turns up eventually to take the situation in hand, and Meursault and Marie return to eat their lunch. Marie, however, has lost her appetite, so that Meursault eats "nearly all" they have prepared.

If not eating signifies unconscious attachment to Mother, eating "nearly all," in this case, suggests unconscious hostility, for Meursault is now thoroughly involved in Raymond's ambivalence. He does not want a policeman to judge the latent pleasure he derives from hearing the Arab girl get what she deserves. ("I agreed it wasn't a bad plan," he said earlier; "it would punish her, all right"). The pleasure, of course, is mixed with guilt and Meursault does not for the moment want to be judged: he wants only to gratify an uncompromising demand from the id. Yet only for the moment. For that Sunday is the day the mistreated dog runs away from the ambivalent Salamano. It's as if the dog's action is for Meursault the appropriate punishment for the unconscious pleasure he has taken in Raymond's sadistic treatment of his mistress. (As well as the pleasure he may have taken in Salamano's brutality towards the dog: when Raymond asks Meursault if he wasn't disgusted by the way the old man served his dog, he answers: "'No.'") It is now clear that his conscious thoughts of his mother ("For some reason, I don't know what, I began thinking of Mother . . .") when he hears Salamano weeping in the next room and his lack of interest in food reveal not only unconscious love, but unconscious hatred and guilt. Ultimately Meursault cannot live without the policeman.

Once it is recognized by the reader that Meursault is a man driven by unconscious forces over which he has little control, the whole novel begins to be a different sort of experience than was intended by the author. It begins to suggest dual, and even multiple perspectives of meaning: not richly, however, but confusingly, for these do not supplement but tend to destroy one another. Unlike Raskolnikov [in Dostoyevsky's *Crime and Punishment*], whose character grows in our mind with the recognition of multiple causation, the strength of Meursault's character is dissipated if there is any possibility of complex and even contradictory motivation. Meursault kills the Arab, he thinks, "because of the sun" just as Raskolnikov kills the old woman to get her money; but Camus tries to give the impression that the sun is a cause for which Meursault is in no way responsible, and that any other deeper causes that the reader may guess at do not concern him, are merely part of society's absurd quest for absolutes. Dostoevsky, on the other hand, *encourages* us to look further and to find a natural continuity between killing for money and the contradictory psychological fact of unconcern about money, between killing for money and killing to prove oneself a moral superman, between killing for money and symbolically killing one's own mother. For Camus there is only *discontinuity* between the sun and any other cause that might imply responsible involvement in society on the part of Meursault: continuity would spoil the picture of an innocent victim. If we dig too deeply into *The Stranger* we destroy the effect that Camus intended to create. Since, nevertheless, we do dig deeply, and cannot help ourselves because Camus himself (unconsciously) encourages us to do so, the effect is spoiled, confusion results, and vital mystery disappears.

THE ULTIMATE MEANING OF MEURSAULT'S SILENCE

The whole novel is filled with clues to Meursault's hidden quest for punishment. The logic of his fate is expressed in his silence. *Sometimes the silence is total:* When the examining magistrate three times asks why he fired four extra shots into the body of the prostrate Arab, Meursault says nothing. At the trial, Meursault at first feels that, he has "something really important to tell" the court, which appears to him to be trying to exclude him from the proceedings, but, "on second thoughts," finds that he has "nothing to say." *Sometimes the silence is not of words but of affect and self-understanding:* Marie seems to shrink away from Meursault's caresses when he tells her that his mother died "Yesterday." "I was just going to explain to her that it wasn't my fault, but I checked myself, as I remembered having said the same thing to my employer, and realizing [sic] then it sounded rather foolish. Still, foolish or not, somehow one can't help feeling a bit guilty, I suppose." Since the bias of the novel urges us to smile at Marie's conventional distaste for someone who fails to pay respects to the dead, and to condemn society's implicit failure to look straight at the truth of mortality, we may be misled by Meursault's casual acceptance of minor guilt and overlook the hint of major unconscious guilt. Again, when Meursault tells the lawyer assigned to defend him that he was "quite fond" of his mother, but then adds, "as an afterthought," that "all normal people . . . had more or less desired the death of those they loved, at some time or another . . . ," the lawyer's worldly-wise response to such simple honesty—he warns Meursault not to make such a statement in court—encourages us to overlook the special relevance of the remark to Meursault's inner life. *Sometimes the silence is neither of words nor affect but of self-understanding:* As Meursault advances alone towards the Arab in the overwhelming heat of the open beach—he feels he must "retrieve the pool of shadow by the rock" and hear the tinkle of the "cold, clear stream behind it—" he is driven to take one, final, fatal step forward, knowing perfectly well that "it was a fool thing to do." But Meursault cannot understand what human force the sun, "pressing on [his] back," signifies. He is not aware of the force of unconscious guilt which demands that society condemn him and execute him.

We smile when the prosecutor proclaims: "'I accuse the prisoner of behaving at his mother's funeral in a way that showed he was already a criminal at heart.'" Even more absurd is the prosecutor's charge that the prisoner is "morally guilty of his mother's death." But both statements express for Meursault his own inexpressible need to collaborate in the punishment which society "absurdly" imposes on him. "It came to this; the man under sentence was obliged to collaborate mentally, it was in his interest that all should go off without a hitch." Meursault is speaking here of how useless it is to wish that the machine would break down—"If by some fluke the knife didn't do its job, they started again"—but he unknowingly testifies to its moral power. In the grand manner of the French tradition, he refuses to accept the moral authority of the guillotine; but what would he do without that knife? It, and not absurdist philosophy, solves Meursault's problem for him.

Thus the novel's unsatisfactory ending, which has been interpreted in many different ways by the critics, cannot be morally justified, but it can, I think, be understood. Meursault, as we have noted, tells the priest that he is not "conscious of any 'sin'" that he has committed, merely that he has performed an anti-social act. But this is precisely why he must irrationally punish himself: he cannot bring his guilt into the light and face himself for what he is. The liberation he experiences after his "great rush of anger" at the priest "had washed me clean" is not—as Camus surely thought it was—so much a sign of achieved philosophical maturity, a lofty awareness of death and its implications, as it is a masochistic satisfaction with his fate. His happy doom now, after having rejected his mother, is to be rejected by his fellow men; yet he must interpret his social condemnation as evidence of his own moral superiority.

Unconsciously, then, Meursault "leaps" to his death, in effect committing not only ordinary suicide but also what Camus calls philosophical suicide, because he needs the moral order of society to which he is consciously indifferent. In *The Myth of Sisyphus* Camus asks: "Is one going to die, escape by the leap, rebuild a mansion of ideas and forms to one's own scale? Is one, on the contrary, going to take up the heart-rending and marvelous wager of the absurd?" Meursault, at bottom, is not really taking up the "wager of the absurd." He is being true to the meaning of his own name. (*meur*: the root of the present indicative of *mourir* 'to die'; suggests also *la mer* 'the sea'; *sault*: related to *sauter* 'to leap,' 'to jump,' and to the English word *sault* 'a leap.') He is leaping to his death, leaping into the maternal sea, rather than continuing to struggle in the gray twilight of the life of the absurd.

CHRONOLOGY

1913

Albert Camus, second son of Lucien Auguste Camus and Catherine Camus (nee Sintès), is born in Mondovi, Algeria, on November 7.

1914

Albert's father is called into military service as World War I breaks out. Albert, together with his mother and brother Lucien (born in 1910), moves to the Belcourt district of Algiers, living with his maternal grandmother, Marie Catherine (née Cardona) Sintès. His father is killed at the first Battle of the Marne on October 11.

1914–1920

Camus's family—including his mother, brother, and two uncles—live with Marie Sintès. His mother works as a charwoman during this time, leaving the brothers to be raised by their disciplinarian grandmother.

1918–1923

Camus attends school and attracts the attention of a teacher, Louis Germain, who helps him gain admission to high school in Algiers despite his grandmother's protests.

1923–1932

Camus wins a scholarship to attend the high school in Algiers, where he plays goalkeeper on the soccer team. Here he meets Jean Grenier, who would remain an influence throughout his life.

1930

Camus contracts tuberculosis and is bedridden for several months.

1931

Camus moves in with his aunt Antoinette and uncle Gustave Acault. Acault strongly encourages Camus's intellectual development in light of his physical problems. Marie Sintès dies.

1932–1933

Camus studies philosophy under Grenier and publishes his first article in a local journal entitled *Sud* (*South*).

1933–1936

Camus attends the University of Algiers and is deeply involved in the antifascism movement on campus.

1934

Camus marries Simone Hié, a morphine addict, on June 16.

1935

Camus begins work on his first book, a collection of short works entitled *The Wrong Side and the Right Side*, finishes his university coursework and begins writing his thesis. He joins the Communist Party in the fall.

1936

Camus helps found the Théâtre du Travail and involves himself fully in its productions. He receives his degree in philosophy but is denied the opportunity to pursue a career in teaching due to his fragile health. He and Simone separate after a trip to Europe.

1937

The Wrong Side and the Right Side is published. Camus leaves the Communist Party because of their lack of support of Muslim Algerians. He founds the Théâtre de L'Equipe. He works as an actor for Radio-Algiers, suffers a relapse of tuberculosis, and takes a trip to Italy, spending most of his time in Florence.

1938

Camus publishes a review of Jean-Paul Sartre's *Nausea*. He starts writing for the new leftist newspaper *Alger-Républicain*. He also begins composing several pieces that will become *The Stranger, The Myth of Sisyphus,* and *Caligula*.

1939

Camus publishes *Nuptials*, a collection of prose poems. He attempts to enlist in the armed forces after World War II breaks out, but he is refused because of his poor health. He writes a number of influential articles of social and political issues in *Alger-Républicain*.

1940

Alger-Républicain is banned by the government in January and ceases publication. At the urging of his friend and former editor Pascal Pia, Camus moves to Paris to work as an editorial secretary for the newspaper *Paris-Soir*. Marries Francine Faure on December 3. He loses his job at *Paris-Soir* soon after the newspaper moves south to Lyon to escape German occupying forces.

1941

Camus and Francine move to Oran, Algeria, where he continues writing and works intermittently as a teacher and as a publisher's reader.

1942

The Stranger is published in July. In August, Camus travels to Le Panelier in south-central France to convalesce after another bout with tuberculosis. He is separated from Francine by military operations in North Africa late in the year.

1943

Camus moves to Paris and begins work as a reader (a job he kept until his death) for his publisher, Éditions Gallimard. Starting late in the year, he writes for the secret Resistance newspaper *Combat*. *The Myth of Sisyphus* is published.

1944

Camus becomes part of a circle of intellectuals that includes Sartre. He meets and has an intense affair with a Spanish actress, Maria Casarès. He is reunited with Francine after the liberation of Paris and becomes the editor of the now openly published *Combat*. His play *The Misunderstanding* is produced for the first time and receives mediocre reviews.

1945

Camus's tuberculosis recurs early in the year. Camus and Francine have twins, Jean and Catherine, on September 5. His play *Caligula* is produced to a mixed reaction.

1946

Camus travels to the United States on a lecture tour. He continues to work with *Combat* and associates closely with Sartre, André Gide, André Malraux, and Arthur Koestler.

1947

The Plague is published and is immediately a great success. Camus leaves his position at *Combat*.

1948

Camus's play *State of Siege* is produced for the first time and almost immediately flops. He resumes his affair with Maria Casarès.

1949

Camus makes a lecture tour of South America. His tuberculosis relapses as a result and he is ill for much of the next two years. His play *The Just Assassins* is produced for the first time.

1950

Actuelles I, a collection of political journalistic pieces, is published while Camus recuperates from illness.

1951

The Rebel is published and is negatively and harshly reviewed by Sartre, which precipitates a permanent end to his friendship with Camus.

1953

Actuelles II is published. Camus begins a three-year period of travel in Italy, Greece, and Algeria that further strains his already rocky marriage. Francine becomes ill during the summer and remains so for more than two years.

1954

Summer, a collection of lyrical essays dating as far back as 1939, is published. Camus becomes directly involved in political turmoil in Algeria.

1956

The Fall is published and receives a warm reception from both readers and critics. Camus adapts William Faulkner's novel *Requiem for a Nun* for the stage. He suffers from continuing health problems. He moves into an apartment of his own, although he and Francine do not legally separate.

1957

Exile and the Kingdom is published. He and Arthur Koestler publish their joint work *Reflections on Capital Punishment.* Camus receives the Nobel Prize in literature.

1958

Camus spends much of the year adapting Dostoyevsky's novel *The Possessed* for the stage. *Actuelles III* is published.

1959

The Possessed is produced for the first time. Camus suffers from severe tuberculosis but works on *The First Man*. He is appointed director of the state-supported experimental theater by his friend and colleague Malraux.

1960

On January 4, Camus is killed instantly in a car wreck near Villeblevin, a town on the outskirts of Paris. His mother dies nine months later.

1970

Simone Hié dies.

1971

An unfinished novel, *A Happy Death*, is published.

1979

Francine Faure dies.

1994

The First Man is published, largely through the efforts of Camus's daughter, Catherine, using a manuscript found at the scene of the accident that killed Camus.

For Further Research

WORKS BY CAMUS READILY AVAILABLE IN ENGLISH TRANSLATION

Between Hell and Reason: Essays from the Resistance Newspaper "Combat", 1944–1947. Trans. Alexandre de Gramont. Middletown, CT: Wesleyan University Press, 1991.

Caligula and Three Other Plays. Trans. Stuart Gilbert. New York: Random House, 1962.

Exile and the Kingdom. Ed. Erroll McDonald. New York: Vintage Books, 1991.

The Fall. Trans. Justin O'Brien. New York: Vintage Books, 1991.

The First Man. Trans. David Hapgood. New York: Vintage Books, 1996.

A Happy Death. Trans. Richard Howard. New York: Vintage Books, 1995.

Lyrical and Critical Essays. Trans. Ellen Conroy Kennedy. New York: Random House, 1995.

The Myth of Sisyphus and Other Essays. Trans. Justin O'Brien. New York: Vintage Books, 1991.

Notebooks, 1935–1951. Trans. Philip Malcolm Waller Thody and Justin O'Brien. New York: Marlowe, 1998.

The Plague. Trans. Stuart Gilbert. New York: Vintage Books, 1991.

The Rebel: An Essay on Man in Revolt. Ed. Erroll McDonald. New York: Vintage Books, 1991.

Resistance, Rebellion, and Death. Trans. Justin O'Brien. New York: Vintage Books, 1995.

The Stranger. Trans. Matthew Ward. New York: Vintage Books, 1989.

Youthful Writings. Trans. Ellen Conroy Kennedy. New York: Knopf, 1976.

FOR FURTHER RESEARCH

Alba Amoia, *Albert Camus.* New York: Continuum, 1989.

Harold Bloom, ed., *Albert Camus.* New York: Chelsea House, 1989.

Germaine Brée, *Camus: A Collection of Critical Essays.* Englewood Cliffs, NJ: Prentice-Hall, 1962.

Hayden Carruth, *After* The Stranger: *Imaginary Dialogues with Camus.* New York: Macmillan, 1964.

John Cruikshank, *Albert Camus and the Literature of Revolt.* Westport, CT: Greenwood Press, 1978.

David R. Ellison, *Understanding Albert Camus.* Columbia: University of South Carolina Press, 1990.

Brian Masters, *Camus: A Study.* London: Heinemann, 1974.

Conor Cruise O'Brien, *Albert Camus of Europe and Asia.* New York: Viking Press, 1970.

Philip H. Rhein, *Albert Camus.* Boston: Twayne, 1989.

Dean Vasil, *The Ethical Pragmatism of Albert Camus: Two Studies in the History of Ideas.* New York: Peter Lang, 1985.

BIOGRAPHIES OF CAMUS

Stephen Eric Bronner. *Camus: Portrait of a Moralist.* Minneapolis: University of Minnesota Press, 1999.

Herbert P. Lottman, *Albert Camus: A Biography.* Garden City, NY: Doubleday, 1979.

Patrick McCarthy, *Camus.* New York: Random House, 1982.

Olivier Todd, *Albert Camus: A Life.* Trans. Benjamin Ivry. New York: Knopf, 1997.

CHRONOLOGICAL LIST OF CAMUS'S PUBLICATIONS

The Wrong Side and the Right Side (1937)
Nuptials (1939)
The Myth of Sisyphus (1942)
The Stranger (1942)
The Misunderstanding (1944)
Caligula (1945)
The Plague (1947)
The State of Siege (1948)
The Just Assassins (1949)
The Rebel (1951)
Summer (1954)
The Fall (1956)
Exile and the Kingdom (1957)
Resistance, Rebellion, and Death (1960)
Notebooks 1935–1942 (1963)
Notebooks 1942–1951 (1965)
A Happy Death (1971)
Youthful Writings (1973)
The First Man (1994)

INDEX